European Guide to TELEWORKING:
A framework for action

EF/94/32/EN

This information booklet was prepared for the Foundation by Solon Consultants of London, U.K. The principal authors are Valerie Bennett and Sheila Moorcroft. Preparation of the booklet text was coordinated in the Foundation by Eberhard Köhler, Research Manager.

Valerie Bennett

Valerie Bennett has been assessing the social impact of new technology and environmental change. In addition, she manages projects and surveys and appraises progress in dynamic fields. Previously, she worked in government research and industrial communications. Her master degrees are in geography (St. Anne's, Oxford) and land resources (Cranfield Institute of Technology), and her earlier publications include "Working at a distance", a study by Solon of tele-commuting and tele-cottages.

Sheila Moorcroft

Sheila Moorcroft has substantial experience of strategic and marketing research, concentrated on the evaluation of technological markets. Past assignments include life-style analysis applied to studies of tele-work; and her earlier research focused on changes triggered by innovations in working practices, and in leisure and shopping behaviour. She has a master's degree in information science and a languages degree, and speaks German fluently. Previously, she worked for SRI International and Taylor Nelson and is now a practising tele-homeworker.

Eberhard Köhler

Eberhard Köhler is presently heading the research programme "Access to Employment, Innovation and Work Organisation" in the European Foundation for the Improvement of Living and Working Conditions. He trained as a political scientist and worked as a lecturer and researcher in the U.S.A., Canada and Germany. In 1988/89 he was visiting research fellow at INSEAD, Fontainebleau, France. He published extensively in several languages on work-organisation issues.

European Guide to TELEWORKING:
A framework for action

by

Sheila Moorcroft
and **Valerie Bennett**

 **European Foundation
for the Improvement of Living
and Working Conditions**
Loughlinstown House,
Shankill, Co. Dublin, Ireland
Tel: +353 1 282 6888
Fax: +353 1 282 6456
Telex: 30726 EURF EI

Cataloguing data can be found at the end of this publication

Luxembourg: Office for Official Publications of the European Communities, 1995

ISBN 92-826-9286-8

© European Foundation for the Improvement of Living and Working Conditions, 1995

For rights of translation or reproduction, applications should be made to the Director, European Foundation for the Improvement of Living and Working Conditions, Loughlinstown House, Shankill, Co. Dublin, Ireland.

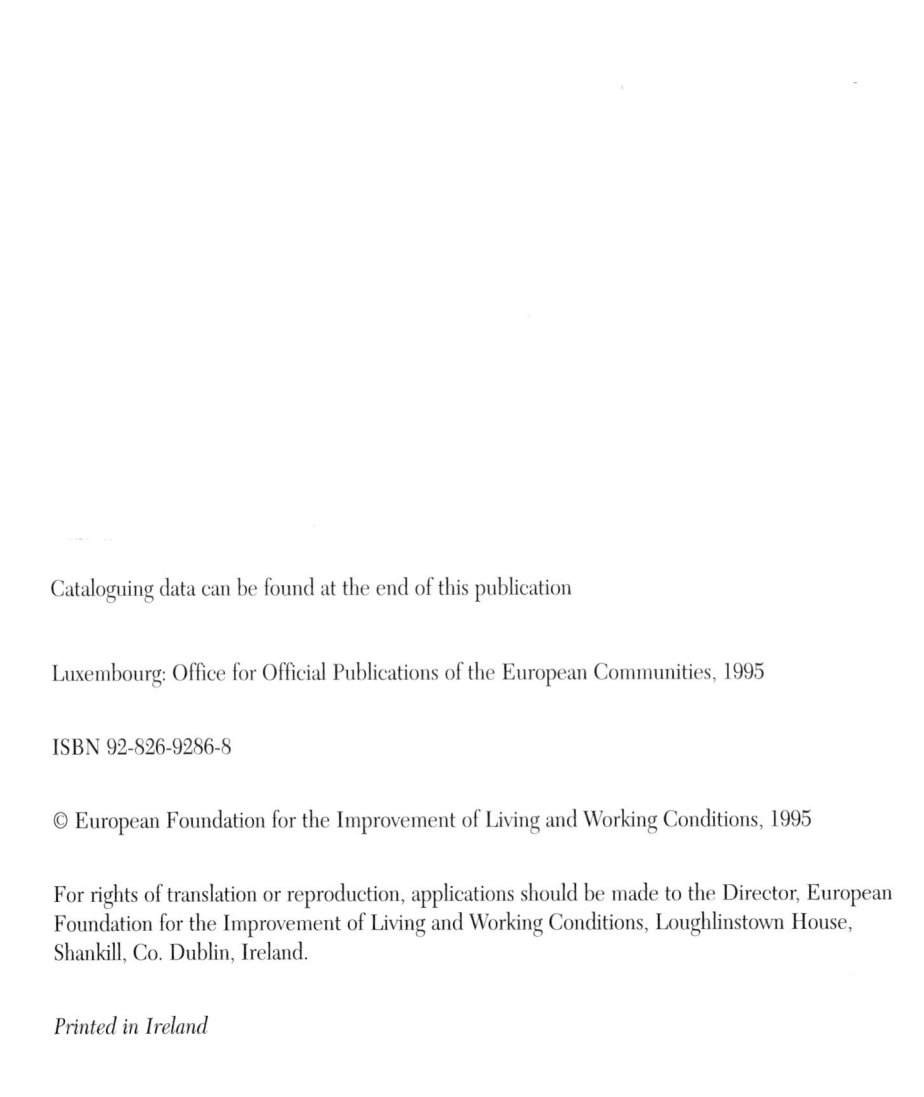

Printed in Ireland

PREFACE

Through its work programme, the Foundation has been building up an understanding of how our societies and economies adjust to new forms of work organisation, to changes in demand for products and services, to new expectations and aspirations, and to continuous technological development.

In recent years, interest in "teleworking" has received increased attention. The Foundation has done research in this field since 1982/83. Many of the research reports had concentrated on discussions of advantages/disadvantages of teleworking. Very few studies had in fact addressed the issue "how to do it in practice". That is what this information booklet is about.

This study is many things at once :

- a practical guide on "good practice"
- a useful guide for managers trying to introduce teleworking in their companies
- a useful guide for the potential teleworker who is contemplating that work form
- a comprehensive cross-national guide, applicable and useful in all the Member States of the European Union.

The emphasis of the report is on a **practical** guide, i.e. a handbook that gives answers to questions of safety and health as much as on more trivial questions of hardware and software selection for the potential free-lance teleworker.

It is complemented by very useful practical tools for evaluating benefits/disadvantages **before** the final decision to do it or not to do it has been taken.

This handbook will meet many people's needs. It is hoped that it will help those interested in teleworking to judge for themselves if this form of work would be suitable for them.

Clive Purkiss, Eric Verborgh
Director *Deputy Director*
October, 1994

ACKNOWLEDGEMENTS

This practical guide to telework is part of the European Foundation for the Improvement of Living and Working Conditions' longstanding and continuing interest in the field of telework dating back to the early 1980's. The current phase of its research programme focuses especially on the impact of telecommunications in the home.

The aim of this guide is to provide an informed starting point and checklist of the issues, benefits and practical steps to home-based teleworking. It has been written with managers, employees and employee representatives in mind.

We could not have compiled the guide alone, and indeed did not. It is the result of discussions with representatives from numerous organisations throughout Europe including organisations currently running telework schemes, consultants specialising in telework implementation, trade unions and government bodies. We would like to extend our heartfelt thanks to all those who were able to take the time to talk to us.

In addition to the discussions we also conducted a detailed review of current European publications, articles and company guidelines on teleworking, a selection of which we have also listed.

CONTENTS

CHAPTER 1:
Introduction 11
Aims and coverage 12
   So, what is telework? 13
      Home-based teleworkers 14
      Neighbourhood work centres 14
      Nomadic staff 14
      Satellite offices 14
A dichotomy 15
Driving forces 16
   Corporate and economic issues 17
   Personal and social concerns 19
   Enabling technologies 19

CHAPTER 2:
Reasons for teleworking 21
Problems looking for a solution 22
The potential benefits: for the employee, the employer and society 25
Areas of concern: for the employee and employer 27

CHAPTER 3:
The steps involved in establishing a teleworking scheme 31
The feasibility study 32
New procedures and selection criteria 33
Awareness and recruitment 34
Final countdown to the pilot scheme 35
Training 35
Evaluating the pilot scheme 36
Formal launch 37

CHAPTER 4:
Selection criteria for successful teleworking 39
The right people 40
The right managers 42
The right jobs 43

CHAPTER 5:
Managing successful teleworking 47
Telework by any other name? 48
Measuring output 49
Job descriptions and responsibilities 50
Processes and guidelines 52
Status and conditions 52
   Employee status 52
   Equal pay, opportunities and conditions 53

CHAPTER 6:
Making the break with the office 55
Is it for you? 56
   How do you see your job? 56
   How office dependent are you? 56
   How self-disciplined are you? 57
   How practical is it? 57

CHAPTER 7:
Thriving on your own 59
Create a barrier 60
Establish the ground rules with the family from the outset 60

Find child-care or elder-care you trust	60
You don't have to be alone	61
Get out of the house at least once a day	61
Give yourself a complete break at lunch time	61
Is there anybody there?	61

CHAPTER 8:
In control and in touch: managing communications 63

From management by osmosis to management by design	64
The phone as a way of life	64
Regular office days	65
Regular daily calls	65
Core contact times	65
Regular departmental/ team meetings	65
Meeting days	66
Telework support groups	66
Social events	66
Staying on the circulation list	67
The company newsletter	67
Telework newsletter	67
An informed centre	68
Trade union access	68
Space implications	68
More meeting rooms	68
Dual use space	68
Quiet rooms for 'hot-desking'	69
Helplines and support	69
A central helpline	69
One-to-one mentors	70
Counselling	70
Technology	70

CHAPTER 9:
Assessing the home as the workplace 73

Definition of a workplace	75
Health and safety	75
Tax	78
Planning regulations	78
Data protection	79
Insurance	79
Running costs	79
Other issues	80

CHAPTER 10:
Defining equipment needs 81

Assessing needs	82
Where to go for help	82
What people have	83
Costs	85
Technical support	85
Data security	86

CHAPTER 11:
Terms and conditions – A summary 89

APPENDICES
Appendix 1

Useful contact addresses	94

Appendix 2

Selected bibliography	101

Appendix 3

Evaluation questionnaires for participants and their managers	107

TABLES:

Table 1
Organisation options: A question of degree 15

Table 2
Interest of employed population in telework by age 18

Table 3
Interest of workstation users in telework by age 18

Table 4
Possible problems for which teleworking may be a solution 23

Table 5
Some potential benefits: for the employee, the employer and society 24

Table 6
Office productivity versus home worker productivity 25

Table 7
Some areas of concern: for the employee and the employer 27

Table 8
Selection criteria for participants 41

Table 9
Manager criteria 43

Table 10
Job characteristics 44

Table 11
Some indicative performance measures and targets 51

Table 12
Home checklist 76

9

Chapter 1

Introduction

The amount of research being conducted into teleworking has led to a much quoted adage that there are more people doing research into telework than there are teleworkers. This may be cynical, but it reflects a growing interest in the field among an ever-widening circle of policy makers, organisations and employees. It is also potentially very misleading, implying as it does that very few people are as yet involved in this form of working.

The European Commission has a directorate responsible for research into teleworking. The French government is actively promoting teleworking as a means of taking work to the country's rural population. German trade unions are negotiating terms and conditions to form the basis of policies and laws governing the implementation of telework. Britain's Department of Trade and Industry and the Department of Employment, at the time of writing, are both financing studies into telework. The popular and business press write about the potential of telework to create a country idyll for the individual, and a flexible, finely tuned workforce for the organisation. The interest is there and growing, so too is the number of practitioners.

So, what is teleworking? What are the steps to take and the issues to address in setting up a scheme? Who will benefit and in what way, and what problems may they encounter? How do you find out more about it?

Aims and coverage

This guide aims to answer those questions. It is written for companies considering implementing a teleworking scheme, and for employees considering whether or not teleworking is a way of life they wish to adopt. The guide is designed as a checklist, to help companies move more easily through the process of considering and setting up a teleworking scheme. It gives detailed lists of issues to take into account when developing a successful teleworking scheme. It includes the regulations, laws and policies that need to be understood, the costs to be considered, the social concerns and requirements that should be addressed.

The steps, selection processes, equipment and training required to establish and manage a successful teleworking scheme are taken into consideration. Solutions to the most frequent anxieties expressed by employees and their managers are given; the unions' concerns and attitudes to teleworking are addressed and possible ways to alleviate them outlined. A range of regulatory and legal issues in the EU are highlighted in relation to health and safety, tax, insurance and contractual considerations. And an extensive list of contacts for each of the major EU countries will help you to obtain more detailed advice and information on the many issues discussed in the guide.

The guide cannot and does not make any pretence of providing a comprehensive coverage of the legal requirements of working conditions or contractual arrangements for teleworking. Nor is it intended to provide all the very detailed information necessary for implementing a teleworking scheme.

What it does provide is a well-informed starting point for anyone, employer or employee, who wants to find out about the practicalities of setting up a telework scheme. It will point you in the right direction; help you to find ways to identify and evaluate the most significant issues which require consideration and research.

So, what is telework?

Telework comes in many guises. It includes both full-time and part-time workers; skilled and unskilled workers. For some people it is a way of life. For others it represents a brief, peaceful interlude from the pressures and interruptions of office life. Teleworkers are as likely to be found in urban areas as in rural ones.

The fundamental difference between teleworking and the current 'norm' is that teleworking schemes take the work to the worker. Employees perform work they would normally do within a conventional office at a different remote location. A variety of telework arrangements has developed to fit companies' needs, ranging from the 'virtual organisation', in which a large number of employees work from home, to the satellite office, which is a remote office of a company.

Home-based teleworkers are the standard bearers of teleworking – they are the virtual organisation. They include employees as well as self-employed people who work at home or from home. Some spend the majority of their time at home, while others divide their time between home and office; others still are based at home but actually spend the majority of their time on the road, in a client's office or, occasionally, in the central office.

Neighbourhood work centres, telecottages, community telework centres or business exchanges, have opened in a variety of locations. In the corporate context they provide local office space for employees who live in the vicinity, thus avoiding the need for a lengthy commute. Many of the other centres aim to bring computing and information-technology training and facilities into small communities. A growing number provide business services from shared office facilities, either operating directly from the centre or using the centre as the hub of a network that incorporates a variety of facilities.

Nomadic staff include people in a wide variety of public and private-sector functions, such as senior managers, sales staff, health visitors and training specialists. The sales executive sends in an order via telephone from a car, on the train or plane; the week's sales report can be compiled at home on a PC, and sent via electronic link to the central office, or a weekly visit can be made to central office. Health visitors send their reports to the relevant doctors, arrange home help, schedule ambulances without having to visit the central health centre.

Satellite offices or back offices, which move administrative or specialist activities away from main sites to take advantage of lower overhead costs or staff availability (or both) have been a growing phenomenon in recent years. Increasingly, such satellite operations are going offshore, for example, to the Caribbean, Ireland and, more recently, to India and Thailand.

Table 1: Organization Options: A Question Of Degree

Home workers	Neighbourhood work centres	Nomadic staff	Satellite offices	Branch offices	Head offices

⟵──────────────────────────────────⟶

The Virtual Organization: Increasing decentralization or fragmentation	The Conventional Organization: increasing centralization

Source: Authors

Telework relies on communications technology to compensate for the remoteness of the worker. This technology may consist of a telephone, PC and the postman; or a highly complex system using broadband networking and groupware. However simple or complex the technology, its function is to allow teleworkers to communicate with their managers, team members or clients and to receive tasks and distribute completed work without leaving their desks. It is the absence of direct supervision, and therefore the changed form of that supervision, which constitutes the most critical difference between teleworkers and conventional office-based workers.

For the purposes of this guide we focus primarily on the issues and actions associated with home-based teleworking, whether it is carried out on a full or part-time basis. Corporate teleworking in neighbourhood or satellite offices will require many of the same considerations in terms of management and design, but none of these issues is quite so extreme as those involved in home-based telework.

A dichotomy

There is a dichotomy: teleworking is both loved and hated. Why? For the advocates it is an effective solution to many of today's problems. It is a means of creating flexible and more competitive organisations. Productivity and quality of output increase when employees become teleworkers. Their quality of life is greatly improved. Advocates believe that telework will regenerate rural areas as work and training opportunities are redistributed to remote areas, and that it will help reduce pollution and environmental degradation, especially in congested cities.

If it offers so much, why do people oppose it? Many managers resist altering the *status quo*, because they do not perceive a need to change, and see significant difficulties in controlling people who are out of sight. Employees fear that once they are out of sight, they will soon be out of mind and eventually out of work. Many trade unions and representative bodies regard teleworking as a retrograde step, mainly because of its associations with the past. Although the concept of teleworking is a recent phenomenon, to some it is a close relation to traditional home-working, sweat-shops or piece-working. Exploitation, low pay and atrocious working conditions were the lot of many before labour laws gave workers rights to a better wage, and better working environments. Some of those who oppose teleworking believe it could mark a return to the bad old days. They also point to some significant issues relating to the potential social and professional isolation which can occur, and indeed, must be addressed.

Driving forces

As already indicated, interest in teleworking and the numbers of people involved are growing. The most significant indicator of this is the growing number of pilot schemes. Financial companies, research and consulting bodies, local government departments and service companies are all examples of organisations adopting a working practice, which was, until recently, the preserve of the information technology sector.

Why should the interest in teleworking be growing now? What are the driving forces behind the growth and the implicit shift of opinion? As with most significant changes in society, a number of trends and developments are combining to create both a need for, and a solution to, change. They divide into three main areas:

❐ corporate and economic issues to which companies need a solution;

❐ social and personal concerns which provide a wider arena for the debate and a catalyst to the process;

❐ enabling technologies for which their developers are actively looking for a market.

Corporate and economic issues

The current structure of work was designed to meet the needs of mass production for which large numbers of people were needed in centralized locations. As we shift from 'brawn power' to 'brain power', with the proportion of information-based jobs in the US and EU workforce already put at over fifty percent and rising, the reasons for us all to work in the same place, at the same time, all the time, disappear.

This change in the nature of jobs is further reinforced by the predicted, forthcoming skill shortages in the EU as the effects of negative or stable birth rates hit the employment market. Companies are looking for more flexible approaches to structuring work, and to keeping their existing staff. They are having to find ways in which to attract different groups of workers, such as women with families who wish to combine raising a family with work, or early retirees who want to continue to work part-time.

The younger generation moving into the workforce are also the first genuine computer generation. Their whole approach to using technology is completely different from those who have learnt to use it, but in many cases have a 'love-hate' relationship with it. This new generation will be much more at ease with, and aware of, its potential. The impact in terms of teleworking is reflected in research by Empirica, which found that interest in working at home was not only significantly higher in four EU countries among the under 40s but even more so among that age group who are already computer users.

Table 2: Interest of Employed Population in Telework by Age

Age	Germany°	France	UK	Italy
15-19	8.5	28.9	28.2	13.3
20-29	11.1	19.9	28.4	13.3
30-39	12.3	15.2	24.6	12.5
40-49	6.9	11.0	19.8	9.6
50-59	3.6	5.7	16.6	8.8
60+	6.9	5.4	~	4.6

° West Germany only   ~ Insufficient data

Source: Huws, U et al; Telework: Towards the Elusive Office

Table 3: Interest of Workstation Users in Telework by Age

Age	Germany°	France	UK	Italy
15-19	10.3	50.0	34.3	24.8
20-29	22.2	32.4	36.7	19.0
30-39	20.9	28.7	36.6	21.0
40-49	10.1	22.5	27.5	21.0
50-59	12.2	19.0	23.1	16.7
60+	~	~	~	~

° West Germany only   ~ Insufficient data

Source: Huws, U et al; Telework: Towards the Elusive Office

As the need to be as competitive as possible increases and cost cutting becomes ever more of a priority, concepts such as telework which are promoted on this basis, and have shown they can deliver, excite attention. High city rents, shortages of key skills in major cities and the mounting costs of congestion in most major EU cities are all fuelling the process.

Personal and social concerns

Quality of life is an increasing focus for many people. To achieve it means having more control over their own destiny, for example, to be able to live where they want to, rather than having to be near their work. Escalating crime, congestion and isolation in many cities are causing an exodus to rural areas as people search for a quieter and safer life for themselves and their families. Teleworking means that they can take their jobs with them. As more people become aware that they have a choice, and that they can combine work more easily with the demands of child- or elder-care, so the demand will increase. Likewise with the needs and aspirations of the disabled who are increasingly unwilling to accept dependence as a way of life. Teleworking, while not the only solution, enhances the range of employment and training options open to people with significant disabilities.

Environmental concern has proved a significant catalyst to telework in the US with the introduction of clean air legislation – for example in Los Angeles. The new legislation requires companies to explore and implement ways of reducing commuter traffic. While similar legislation is not proposed in the EU, environmental concerns and city air quality are firmly on the agenda, and we may yet see legislation.

Rural regeneration is a significant issue for many EU countries and a major policy area for the European Commission. Telework is being explored as a means of providing jobs and developing the skill base in rural areas throughout the community.

Enabling technologies

Technological advances alone are not and never will be sufficient to promote change, but without the new technologies teleworking could not be contemplated. Telephones and PC's are the linchpins of teleworking, but it is the upgrading of the one, with the introduction of ISDN and satellite communications, coupled with the increasing power:price ratio of the other that has opened up new horizons. The need for people to congregate in the same place rapidly diminishes if all the other recent developments are added to the equation, such as much faster Group 3 (increasingly Group 4) facsimile machines; mobile phones and pagers; genuinely portable, rather than luggable, PC's; e-mail and voice mail facilities.

The upgrading of the telecommunications network using new technology such as the introduction of fibre optics means that our ability to transmit vast amounts of data, to send high definition images electronically and to create moving images from CD ROMs and videos, will become a reality. This will pave the way for the technologies which have been waiting in the wings, such as teleconferencing and videophones, to make meetings across the airwaves a reality. Not far behind will come groupware which will enable us to work together on the same document or on graphic images. Each will see the same image and the same real time alterations. These technologies will of course never completely remove the need to meet face-to-face, just as the phone has not. They will however enhance our ability to work together in new ways.

The majority of teleworking schemes are grafted onto existing conventional corporate structures, and were adopted to solve particular problems within organisations. As organisations continue to look for ways of improving their performance, and the technology continues to develop apace, teleworking will become part of the new structure.

Chapter 2

Reasons for teleworking

Just as there is no single definition of teleworking, there is no such thing as a standardized teleworking scheme. The aims and objectives of the scheme, the culture of the organisation, the people and departments involved, the families of the teleworkers, the nature of the work, the country in which the company is operating, will all affect the way in which the scheme is set up and run. That said, there are a number of key concerns, approaches and questions which are central to telework and need to be highlighted.

Implementing change is never an easy task. It requires time, effort and commitment. Implementing a teleworking scheme is no exception. It requires:

❐ a good reason for adopting it, to provide impetus, overcome inertia, motivate people and help counter a natural tendency to resist change; either because of problems which need addressing, or there is dissatisfaction with the *status quo*.

❐ a vision of what the end result will look like and the benefits for those concerned which will help people to identify with the process, gain their commitment, give them a sense of direction, and so help them to chart new territory successfully and understand why the effort is worthwhile;

❐ a clear idea of the steps involved, the resources required and the problems which need to be addressed to enable everyone to assess progress, achieve the end result with as little disruption as possible and to know when an effective solution has been achieved.

Problems looking for a solution

It is essential to identify the reasons for considering teleworking from the outset. First and foremost the business case for changing the *status quo* should be defined. This should calculate the costs and assess the potential benefits. This will also help to define the type of scheme which is suitable. For example, if staff retention is an issue, and employees have long and difficult commutes, then a predominantly home-based scheme with full

Table 4: Possible problems for which teleworking may be a solution

Personnel Issues
- High staff turnover
- High proportion of women staff
- Growing numbers of employees with children/elderly care responsibilities
- Potential skill shortage in strategically significant areas
- Sick leave problems
- Recruitment problems
- Increased concerns and complaints about commuting
- Risks to employees in 'no-go' parts of the city, as they travel to and from work

Space Issues
- Need more space for expansion
- Need less space because nature/amount of work has changed
- End of current lease
- Relocation/office move under consideration
- Major office refurbishment needed
- Overheads increasing significantly
- High proportion of desks empty at any one time

Work related issues
- Complaints about interruptions
- Growing numbers of people already work at home on an informal basis
- Most work project-based
- Significant peaks and troughs in workload
- Management concern re office productivity

Table 5: Some potential benefits:

For the employee
- More control over work environment.
- More flexibility about timing and structure of work.
- Less commuting and so more time and money, less stress.
- More flexibility about where to live.
- Closer integration of home and work.
- Enhanced skills.
- Improved job satisfaction.
- Improved quality of life.
- Allows a gradual return to work after sickness or injury.
- More independence for the disabled.

For the employer
- Radically improved productivity among teleworkers.
- Improved staff retention.
- Reduced overheads and labour costs.
- Improved quality of work.
- Reduced absenteeism.
- Greater flexibility in work patterns.
- Improved 24 hour technical support/customer care.
- Wider staff recruitment area.
- Increased skill base in company.
- More explicit knowledge of job content, workload and output.
- Speedier return to work after sick leave.
- Improved management skills.
- Global 24 hour operations without attendant anti-social work hours.

For society
- Less pollution.
- Less congestion in cities.
- Reduced energy consumption.
- Improved employment for rural areas.
- Reduced healthcare costs.
- Greater community identity and focus.
- More employment opportunities for the disabled.
- Regeneration of old industrial communities.

employee status would be appropriate. If they tend to live in the same area, a neighbourhood office might be a solution. If, on the other hand, some of the people likely to leave are doing so to set up their own business, then a scheme based partially on self-employed status might be best. By identifying and assessing the problems which need changing, you are also beginning to establish your current position, which is essential if you are to measure progress to your goal.

The potential benefits: for the employee, the employer and society

While there is a range of problems for which teleworking may be a solution, it may not be the only solution. What are the additional benefits of teleworking for the individual, the organisation and society at large, which may make telework a more appropriate solution than any other?

The extent to which any of these benefits applies will again vary from company to company and person to person. However, in the schemes

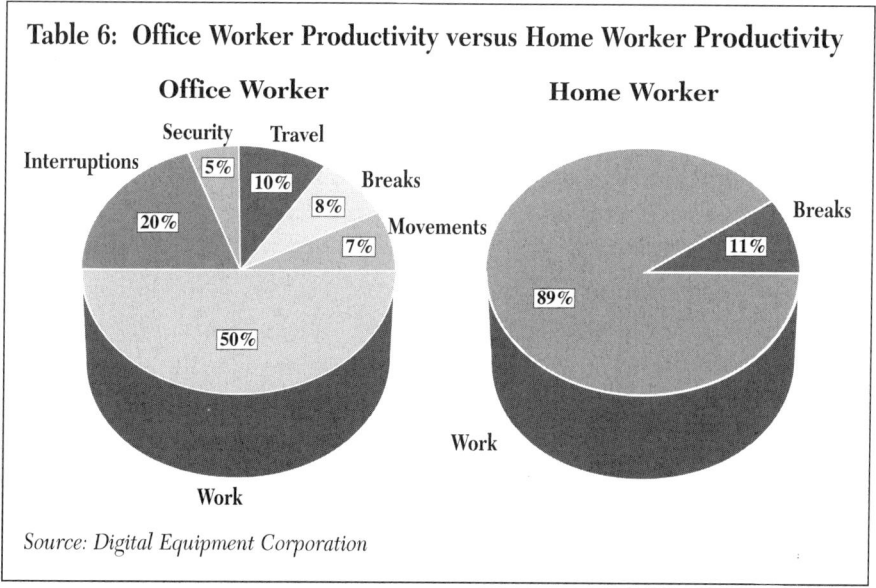

Table 6: Office Worker Productivity versus Home Worker Productivity

Source: Digital Equipment Corporation

which are running to date, all of these benefits have been identified in some or all instances.

For the individual the benefits tend to be focused very much on the more tangible areas of improved quality of life, although there are undoubted benefits in terms of the sense of achievement that arises from improved productivity and control over one's destiny. There appears also to be a slightly different emphasis in perceived benefits between the sexes. Women tend to regard the opportunity to integrate their dual responsibilities of job and family as a greater benefit than do men. For men, the benefits remain centred around their improved ability to work effectively and to be more in control of their own destiny, although it must be said that they too recognise the benefits of having more time at home with the family.

The most significant benefits are productivity increases, staff retention and recruitment, and reduced costs and overheads. Productivity increases of 30 to 40 percent among teleworking staff are regularly reported. Digital estimate that productive work time rises from 50 percent to 89 percent when employees move from office-based work to home-based work. Those who are not directly involved with telework often underestimate the growth in productivity and some may even be unaware of this potential benefit.

Staff retention was the single most significant benefit for 21 percent of companies which participated in a recent NCC survey in the UK, and a significant benefit to a further 51 percent. The employee circumstances will vary but include women with children, people wishing to be independent, those wishing to retire, those with elderly care responsibilities, those wishing to move to a more remote area, or who need to move because of a partner's job. Again, in more isolated instances, employees who suffer serious accidents or illness may be able to return to work relatively quickly when able to work from home for short periods during recuperation. Where the resulting problems are more debilitating, it may be the only long term solution to retaining their services.

Staff retention has so far been more important than staff recruitment because of the perceived need for work experience and a track record with the company. However, recruitment benefits are increasing, as some schemes are now successfully drawing on new pools of employees, many of whom have never worked within the conventional job market.

The benefits of increased productivity and a reduction in costs and overheads will be felt by the organisation over a period of time, but only once the up-front costs of setting up the scheme have been met. Substantial savings will only be made if large numbers of employees become teleworkers and the organisation is therefore able to close an office, or no longer needs to relocate to larger premises. Digital, for example, in the aftermath of a major office fire were able to carry out the same operations with the same numbers of staff from an office half the size of the original building, by extending their teleworking scheme.

Table 7: Some areas of concern:

For the employee	*For the employer*
• Loss of employee status, protection, benefits and pay.	• Remote management, control, communication, logistics.
• Isolation – social and professional.	• Security and confidentiality of information and systems.
• Reduced career opportunities.	• Team and company identity and loyalty.
• Less interesting work, and increased monotony.	• Costs.
• Loss of home/work distinction, and increased stress.	• Time required to plan and implement.
• Increased home related costs.	• Child/elder-care to ensure adequate undisturbed work time.
• Health and safety standards and implementation.	
• Child/elder-care.	• Start up costs.
• Employee representation/union membership.	• Running costs.

The costs of setting up a scheme, equipping and training staff are considerable and the reduction in the need for office space is often less than anticipated because of the need to provide meeting rooms and quiet space when teleworkers are in the office. It was, nevertheless, perceived as being the single most important benefit by 27 percent of companies and a significant benefit for 53 percent in the NCC survey.

Areas of concern: for the employee and employer

Teleworking is not without its potential problems and these areas of concern need to be addressed, both for the protection of the individual, and for the successful management of the work and people involved. Most of them can be avoided – or at the very least, reduced to a manageable level by careful design and planning. Much of the debate about the potential, acceptability and likely long term development of teleworking has focused on these issues.

For the individual, the areas of concern centre around the loss of opportunity and the potential for exploitation which working away from the office seems to represent, coupled with and reinforced by the practicalities and complexities of being on their own. The recommendations concerning training, support, procedures, terms and conditions and overall management of telework schemes are designed, not only to alleviate such problems, but to prevent them arising in the first place.

For management, the central issues are the loss of face-to-face contact and communication, which lead to the perceived problems of a lack of managerial, motivational and disciplinary control over the workforce. These problems, plus the costs in terms of time and money of setting up and running a teleworking scheme, are the prime reasons for telework not gaining support. These are without doubt significant issues. But they are not without solution.

A management approach based on trust with clearly defined, measurable outputs creates the necessary basis for teleworking. This approach has the additional benefit of providing far greater knowledge and understanding about the work being done both by teleworkers and their managers.

The wider implications of inaction are often not taken into consideration in cost analysis. For example, the direct and indirect costs of replacing valuable and highly skilled long term members of staff can far outweigh the costs of setting up a teleworking scheme, even for only a few people. A telework scheme may also save the costs of relocating and provide a reduction in overheads by transferring administration to a low cost office area or where there is a greater pool of relevant staff. The significant productivity gains will also usually more than offset the start-up costs incurred.

The unions were originally almost unanimous in their rejection of teleworking. Their concern focused on the potential exploitation of employees and a return to the bad old days of homeworking and its association with piece-rates, poor pay and conditions, plus the dangers of social isolation. But some European trade unions such as STE and Deutscher Gewerkschatsbund are now not only actively negotiating with employers to ensure the best possible terms and conditions for employees, but in many respects are more open to these changes than some of the managers they are negotiating with. Success will be easier to achieve where it is a joint effort.

The terms and conditions discussed later, especially in chapter 10, address these and the other areas of concern listed in Table 7. These recommendations are distilled from a wide variety of organisations currently involved in teleworking.

Chapter 3

The steps involved in establishing a teleworking scheme

There are six essential stages to setting up a successful teleworking scheme, each of which is discussed briefly below:

- ❐ Conducting a detailed feasibility study;
- ❐ Developing new procedures and selection criteria;
- ❐ Creating awareness and recruiting potential participants;
- ❐ Designing and launching the pilot scheme;
- ❐ Evaluating the pilot scheme;
- ❐ Formally launching the final programme.

The feasibility study

The objectives of the feasibility study are fourfold:

• to develop a business case for implementing a telework scheme. This will identify and quantify any of the potential problems listed earlier for which telework may be a suitable solution. The business case should then focus on one or two main issues to be addressed, in particular, highlighting the costs of not taking action, as well as the projected, potential savings.

• to gain top management commitment and support at board level, especially if they have not initiated the idea. This support is essential – without it the scheme will never succeed. This should include an articulate, board-level champion.

• to identify all the issues and concerns which need to be addressed, so that the scheme will balance the needs of the organisation as a whole, including the management involved in running the scheme and the individuals who will work remotely.

• to assess the overall potential for telework, including departments/people with appropriate jobs/the level of interest.

New procedures and selection criteria

Before developing the actual scheme, clear ground rules are needed. You will need to have defined:

- the terms and conditions of participation;
- the selection criteria for participants and their supervisors;
- the likely training needs of all concerned;
- the support systems for people once they are teleworking;
- the time and communications structure within which the scheme will function;
- the equipment needs, costs and related issues such as maintenance, insurance and control of use;
- any legal and regulatory issues relating to tax, local planning regulations, health and safety etc.

All these must be tailored as closely as possible to the needs of the individual department and organisation. However, rather than reinvent the wheel, there is a wealth of information and experience to draw on. Chapter 4 summarizes some of the core criteria and guidelines. There is also a growing number of organisations which provide consulting services for the design of telework schemes over and above the conventional personnel, computer and information technology consulting organisations, all of which could provide additional assistance. Some are listed in Appendix A.

The personnel department and the managers involved will still need to conduct detailed research. This will ensure that local tax, planning, legal, and health and safety regulations are complied with. Employee representatives should be involved from the outset to ensure that they are satisfied with the terms and conditions and do not regard the scheme as a means for exploitation. They should also help to define their own needs and objectives, both for designing the framework for the day-to-day running of the scheme and the criteria for assessing progress and success.

Awareness and recruitment

Potential participants who satisfy the criteria for teleworking, both in terms of their personal characteristics and job suitability, will need detailed information and time for discussion to understand the aims, benefits and potential problems that might arise from teleworking.

It is also important to explain to individuals for whom teleworking is not an option, for whatever reason, why this is the case. This avoids resentment building up if teleworking is seen as a perk that is being withheld, rather than a work option that is simply not practicable for them.

There are a number of options for generating interest, enthusiasm, involvement and commitment to the idea of a teleworking scheme. As already mentioned, a visible, high level, preferably board level, champion of the scheme, who will provide a focus and identity to the scheme from the outset, is a must. The publicity then needs to start, providing a broad sweep introduction of the idea, followed up by increasingly focused and detailed meetings and discussions. The first phase of publicity should include the publication of articles in the company newspaper, question and answer sessions with key representatives, and general circulars and memos outlining the concept and giving information about who may or may not be eligible, and what steps they need to take if they are interested.

The more focused assessments will then require a detailed questionnaire for all prospective participants and managers covering the following:

- personal qualities needed by successful teleworkers and their managers;
- job criteria;
- manager criteria;
- analysis of tasks and time spent on different activities;
- the type of communication and information teleworkers need to do their jobs;

- time, distance and problems encountered in commuting;
- reasons for participants' interest;
- home and personal circumstances;
- concerns, or problems which may be encountered.

These will be followed up by discussions with personnel and the supervisors concerned.

The final result will produce a small group of participants in the pilot scheme. They will not only be willing volunteers, happy to be guineapigs, but will be actively committed to the idea. They will be suitable candidates who have willing and supportive managers and supervisors. In other words, there should be as strong a bias for success as possible.

Final countdown to the pilot scheme

Having found willing and able participants, it is now time to train and equip them ready for the launch. Training is essential. Teleworking is a culture shock, however well suited to coping and benefiting from it participants may be. Moving from being in a conventional and familiar workplace to working successfully elsewhere, and on your own for at least some of the time, does not happen overnight.

Training

The profiling exercise for selecting people will have provided important information concerning any gaps in their skills which may need to be developed. Assuming that participants have good general professional skills for their own work, training will still need to cover:

- a review of the teleworking scheme, its aims and objectives, and the measures of success;
- new management skills – time management, project management, negotiation and assertiveness, stress management, administrative and basic business skills, and home practicalities;

- formal and informal communication skills – written, oral and electronic – for managers and employees;
- technical skills relating to the use of equipment and networks;
- rights and responsibilities relating to both setting up at home and day-to-day work practices;
- an awareness of health and safety procedures.

Managers as well as participants need to take part in the orientation process. This will ensure that everyone involved not only has a shared understanding of what is involved and how to proceed, but also helps to develop a stronger group identity. In addition the group has an opportunity to provide mutual advice and support from the outset. This is especially important if participants come from different departments.

Other tasks, most of which are discussed in more detail in later chapters, include:

- installing the necessary equipment in participants' homes;
- finalizing and signing contracts and agreements;
- setting up helplines and communication systems to ensure that participants have as much support and advice on hand as possible – especially in the early days of the scheme;
- defining individual timetables and work patterns;
- ensuring that all legal, regulatory and safety related issues have been dealt with;
- setting a date for the launch;
- designing the evaluation process.

Evaluating the pilot scheme

The evaluation process must take place before, during and after the main pilot project. It needs to take into account:

- how managers and participants feel the experiment is proceeding; attitudes to it and how these change over time, benefits and problems anticipated but not encountered and vice versa;
- time required for different types of activity;
- specific output measures for the work being done with, if possible, the same measures being applied to any staff continuing to work under 'normal' conditions;
- detailed records of costs and savings – primarily communication costs but also travel, heating and lighting, catering and any other practical day-to-day costs incurred, or avoided, directly as a result of teleworking;
- regular review sessions with participants;
- publicity about the scheme for the rest of the organisation;
- designing and ensuring an unbiased escape route for a return to office-based working for those who find, contrary to expectation, that teleworking is simply not for them;
- final presentation of findings to the board.

Formal launch

Once the evaluation report has received board approval, the pilot scheme can be formalized, and systems and procedures set in place for its expansion. This, again, needs detailed discussion and publicity on a par with, if not greater than, that for the pilot project, since teleworking will now start to become an official part of company practice – albeit a voluntary one.

The selection criteria, procedures and guidelines etc, will all need to be incorporated into company policy documents. Many of the techniques developed specifically for the teleworking scheme may also provide an important framework for new procedures within office-based departments. Targets and procedures for expanding the scheme will also need to be developed.

Chapter 4

Selection criteria
for successful
teleworking

A successful teleworking scheme displays five fundamental characteristics. These are: voluntary participation; a strong culture of trust; open, two-way communications; clear ground rules established from the outset and the right people. None of these occurs by chance: they are the result of the preparations outlined in the previous chapter.

In this chapter we will discuss the content of those procedures, the criteria for selection and the issues which need addressing in more detail. Our conclusions are drawn from an analysis of:

- ❏ Published research and literature;

- ❏ Questionnaires and agreements used by European companies currently operating teleworking schemes;

- ❏ Indepth interviews conducted with company and union representatives throughout Europe.

The right people

Finding the right people is the key to successful teleworking. No amount of planning, enthusiasm or careful job definition can make up for a lack of suitable candidates. It is important to remember that not even all those who are willing and interested in the idea may be suitable. To avoid costly, disruptive mistakes careful selection is essential. A mistake could leave an individual feeling demoralized and a failure.

The selection process has several stages: identifying the general level of interest, profiling the most likely candidates in more detail and then the final selection. This will involve a combination of self-assessment questionnaires to be filled in by potential candidates and their supervisors, and interviews with the personnel managers and with the departmental manager or supervisor. Some companies use professional profiling and selection services to assist in the development and administration of tests, and specialist telework services are now developing.

Table 8 : Selection criteria for participants

Personal characteristics	Work related attitudes/skills	Personal circumstances
• Flexible;	• Able to work unsupervised and without peer pressure;	• Adequate space at home;
• Reliable;		• Suitable child/elder-care;
• Adaptable;		
• Trustworthy;	• Good communication skills;	• Friends/social life outside the workplace;
• Focused;		
• Self-disciplined;		
• Confident;	• Good people skills;	• Supportive family;
• Sensible;	• Professional approach;	• Desire/reason for change.
• Independent;		
• Self starter;	• Well organized;	
• Team player.	• Good time management;	
	• Good at problem solving;	
	• Good track record time keeping/sick leave/ meeting deadlines;	
	• Experience of the job;	
	• Several years' experience with the organization;	
	• Technically *au fait*.	

The final decision about who is, or is not, eligible to telework should lie with the immediate supervisors or managers concerned, since they will be responsible for the performance and well-being of the staff in question.

Candidates should display many, if not all, of the characteristics listed in table 8. These fall into three overall categories – personal attributes, work related attitudes and skills, and personal circumstances – all of which are closely related. Candidates should also be willing to participate in the scheme and want to change their working practices, whether for personal, family, work, or commuting reasons.

It is also important to remember that people who are well suited to teleworking may not necessarily be those performing best under normal office circumstances. There have been examples of people who have needed regular periods of sick leave caused by job-related stress and a lengthy commute, but who once they were established on a teleworking scheme have needed almost no time off for sick leave.

Regular interruptions which inevitably occur in the office affect the performance of people involved in work requiring long periods of concentration. Some people will be affected more than others. By becoming teleworkers, such people may find their productivity and quality of work increases as interruptions decrease.

The right managers

Most of the arguments against teleworking stem from management concern. Some managers are concerned about their perceived loss of control over their staff. Managers involved in the scheme will, therefore, also need to be assessed for their suitability. While the criteria are not necessarily as extensive as those for people working remotely, there are some characteristics managers need to have without which a project will never succeed. First and foremost is, again, a willingness and desire to participate. In some schemes the managers themselves are, or have been, teleworkers and are, therefore, better able to understand and fully

> **Table 9: Manager criteria**
> - Trust in their staff;
> - Ability to set clear objectives and delegate;
> - Project management skills for scheduling and timetabling work;
> - Good communication skills – formal and informal, written and oral;
> - Good at motivating staff and encouraging independence and initiative;
> - Flexibility about time use – even under conventional office circumstances;
> - Good at providing feedback and assessment of performance;
> - Output oriented – rather than process oriented – management

appreciate the problems and concerns of their staff. But this is not essential. There are many schemes which operate successfully where the manager has always been based in the office.

Employees and their managers participating in a teleworking scheme usually increase their skill base which may be enhanced by further training. Monitoring and quantifying these improvements provides valuable information for the evaluation programme, as well as enabling a more focused assessment of participants in the future. Indeed, if any kind of objective measures of success are to be developed, then consistent and measurable criteria for the people involved are essential.

The right jobs

Assessing the people for their suitability must go hand in hand with assessing their jobs. Participants will need to qualify on both counts. There is little point in having a highly trustworthy and independent receptionist if they are not at the front desk to greet visitors!

Table 10: Job characteristics
- High information content in at least part of the job;
- Low need for frequent, face-to-face, unscheduled communication;
- High need for extended periods of concentration;
- Personal flexibility and control over pace and timing of actual periods of work;
- Clearly defined outputs;
- Discrete, identifiable milestones and targets;
- Low need for access to non-electronic information or equipment;
- Low space requirements for storage and equipment;
- Low need for highly confidential or sensitive information.

The growth in information-based jobs has been one of the key drivers of the growth of teleworking. Information-based work, however, spans a wide spectrum – from straightforward data entry tasks to software development and consultancy. Not all are appropriate, indeed only an estimated 25 percent of all current information-based jobs are suitable. So, if information is the basic ingredient, what are the others?

Most jobs are easily broken down into their key activities, for example, planning, analysis, design and report writing. This helps to make the analysis and assessment of particular jobs relatively easy. Since very few jobs consist of only one activity, prospective participants may need to keep a time-log of the activities which their job entails to identify discrete elements which are suited to remote working, even if not all of their work is. The job assessment process may also need detailed interviews by the personnel department to identify other tasks and skills required to do the job.

To date, teleworking has focused primarily at the more complex, professional, skilled end of the information spectrum. But there is also a growing number of schemes targeting the clerical end of the spectrum such as data entry and telephone enquiry services. The range of jobs suitable for telework will increase as experience of running and managing telework schemes increases, and the technology for providing more realistic remote communication improves.

Chapter 5

Managing successful teleworking

So far we have been looking primarily at the preparations for teleworking. Chapter 4 highlights some of the considerations that influence the selection of managers for teleworking schemes. We need now to focus more closely on some of the management issues involved in actually running a scheme, the problems that may arise and some possible solutions to those problems.

Managing teleworkers does not require any specially designed techniques: carefully thought through best practice is usually enough. That best practice, however, does need to incorporate:

- ❐ output orientation with measurable targets;
- ❐ clearly defined responsibilities and job descriptions;
- ❐ well publicized processes and procedures;
- ❐ excellent communications;
- ❐ forward planning.

Sadly, it is the absence of many of these considerations which has led to the perception that management equates with close, physical supervision. If managers rely on informal acquisition of information, and organise unscheduled and perhaps even ill-planned meetings, staff will necessarily have to be constantly present in the office. Such management practice will not allow the implementation of a successful teleworking scheme.

Telework by any other name?

Within most organisations at least one department already displays many of the key characteristics of teleworking, but no one calls it that: the sales department. Sales staff spend most of the time away from their desks and the office. They work on the move, at or from any number of locations including home, the car, trains and planes, hotels, customers' offices. They need to stay in regular contact with the office and usually do so through regular call-ins, meetings and centralized schedules of customer calls. Output and performance are clearly defined and measurable with target numbers of calls to be achieved, call-to-sale conversion rates and revenue targets. To do their job well sales staff need to be highly motivated and identify strongly with the organisation.

Many of these characteristics can be found in peripatetic groups, such as maintenance staff with responsibility for widely dispersed equipment, or health visitors with a heavy case load of calls.

Measuring output

Some jobs are easier than others to convert to output orientation, but none is impossible. Unfortunately, what cannot be measured is usually deemed not to exist. Measures of some sort therefore need to be found, even for such difficult concepts as quality or customer satisfaction.

Project-based activities lend themselves very readily to output orientation since they have clearly defined parameters which include customers' requirements, outputs/deliverables expected, timetables and deadlines. Keeping track of who has done what, when and to budget is very straightforward. Such activities also have a built-in combination of short and longer term targets against which to monitor progress and so identify problems early on.

Continuous activities such as information processing, data entry, accounts, word processing, can also be assessed by output. But here the spectre of piece-rates and exploitation rises; hence the union resistance to telework. Targets may be much shorter term, weekly or even daily, relying on basic information about the number of accounts processed, pages typed, etc. Again, under-performance can highlight problems at an early stage and allow for timely action, for example, warnings, training, sick leave.

Both these options are fairly tightly controlled and monitored. A third option for very independent employees is to define a longer term objective or task, agree a deadline and leave the teleworkers to it. A deadline focuses the mind, and the employees for whom this is an appropriate option usually welcome the freedom of choice and total control that they are given.

If deadlines focus the mind, performance measures provide peace of mind for all parties. Everyone knows what is expected and when it has been achieved. While it can serve to highlight early signs of difficulties, output orientation can also mean that high performers receive recognition and, if goals are achieved in less time, they can also have some time off.

Setting targets and performance measures must be a collaborative process. A fine line has to be taken between encouraging good performance and demotivating employees by overstretching them.

- targets need to be realistic and allow for a range of acceptable achievement;
- targets need to allow room for manoeuvre and some variety in the tasks. Monotony is one of the dangers of teleworking, especially in the more routine, information processing jobs;
- flexibility of work times is a significant benefit for many teleworkers, especially for women 'returners', who have child-care responsibilities. Targets need to enable them to schedule work accordingly.

Productivity increases are one of the main benefits for employers, and most people want to do good work, if given the chance and motivation. Unrealistic targets and poor management will only demotivate teleworkers and lead ultimately to the failure of the scheme.

Job descriptions and responsibilities

If job descriptions were not detailed enough before embarking on a teleworking scheme, they should be by now. Assessing the jobs for teleworking may have had the knock-on effect of identifying previously inadequate definitions of roles, functions and responsibilities throughout an organisation. If nothing else came out of the process, that would be a significant benefit, as long as the necessary action is taken!

As already indicated, many of the new responsibilities for teleworkers are not unlike those of running a small business – especially in connection

Table 11: Some indicative performance measures and targets

Sales force	Calls per day
	Calls-to-sale conversion rate
	Monthly/quarterly revenue
Training	Active training days
	Revenue generated
	Repeat business by department/external client
	New methods and courses developed
Word Processing	Documents/pages typed
	Number of mistakes not picked up by the employee
	Type of document capable of processing – text, graphics etc
Customer Satisfaction	Amount of repeat business
	Number of complaints
	Time delay in meeting order/call
Quality	Number of faults
	Response times
	Level of accuracy

Source: Authors/Burch, S; *Teleworking*. These are also measures which provide part of the basis for the evaluation of the pilot scheme as well as the basis for its long-term management.

with wider issues such as health and safety etc. The training sessions for teleworkers should have clarified these, but the more job-specific responsibilities will need to be discussed as part of the review and assessment process.

Processes and guidelines

Again, most of the general procedures and guidelines will have emerged from the assessment and design phases and should have stemmed from the organisation's existing procedures manual. They should be discussed as part of the training sessions, and clear, easy-to-read documentation of the key points provided. Where to go for more detailed advice and support should also be clearly stated, and the necessary helplines set in place.

Status and conditions

Teleworking is frequently discussed in connection with the wider debate about flexibility and cost cutting, and indeed can provide both benefits. The concept of the core and the peripheral workforce has been a significant factor in these discussions, causing the unions grave concern about the status, pay and employment security of their members and the wider workforce.

These concerns, together with company/union agreements and detailed discussion with current practitioners, have formed the basis for the summary terms and conditions in the last chapter of the guide. Companies and unions throughout Europe are now collaborating to develop detailed agreements and guidelines concerning the full range of terms and conditions associated with teleworking. This collaboration in defining the basis of the scheme is essential to its success and has been a very significant aspect of the IBM experimental teleworking project in Germany. There, a comprehensive agreement has been finalized to ensure maximum rights and protection for employees, to clarify and define their responsibility and to provide managers with the frame of reference within which to manage their staff.

Employee status

The unions' concern is not without foundation. Greater flexibility for one usually means less security for another, and there has been a general shift towards short-term contracts, self-employment and sub-contracting. Part-time work has also been on the increase reflecting the growing number of working mothers. It also provides work opportunities to women for whom conventional full-time work is not an option. It is against this background that the unions have been anxious to establish full employee status as the norm, especially for part-timers. They also want to guarantee full access to benefits such as sick leave and holiday entitlements – albeit on a *pro-rata* basis. Guarantees of statutory maternity leave, unemployment benefit, procedures and length of notice for dismissal, etc. are also key areas of concern.

Equal pay, opportunities and conditions

Research has shown that many teleworkers are less well paid, even when pro-rated to allow for part-time employment. They often feel that they receive the less interesting and less challenging jobs, even in the professional areas such as programming. Hence the need to guarantee equal pay and conditions, career development and training for all teleworkers.

Chapter 6

Making the break with the office

Is it for you?

The company is ready to accept new working practices. The management is keen to initiate a pilot telework scheme. The support structure is in place. All that's needed now are the teleworkers. Should you volunteer? Could you cope? What issues should you consider before launching yourself into a whole new way of working?

Although you and your immediate manager will discuss what is involved, you will still need to ask yourself whether or not teleworking is for you, especially if you are to work primarily at or from home. It may be easier to be honest with yourself if you have a few pointed questions to answer in private. Ultimately, it is not just the rational, practical aspects of working from home which are important, but whether it feels right for you. These questions will help you to pause and think along slightly different lines about the decision.

How do you see your job?
This is not so much a question of whether your career opportunities may be affected by teleworking, which they should not be, but how you feel about your work and its importance in terms of who and what you are. How will you cope with other people's possible perceptions that working from home is 'odd' or 'not a proper job'? How much of your identity is tied up in what you do for a living? Do you actively want to change the balance between home and work to give greater emphasis to home and leisure? What are the pros and cons – make a list. How does it feel? What is your gut reaction when you imagine being at home most of the time? Do you like being different?

How office dependent are you?
This is more about the social aspects of office life than it is about the formal aspects of being at work, although those too are important. Do you like to know what is going on all the time, and to be able to hear and pass

on information on the grapevine? Are office politics an important part of your enjoyment of work? Are most of your friends and social activities connected with your work? Do you see friends at the beginning and end of the work day? Do you tend to keep yourself to yourself while at work or do you want to be where the action is?

How self-disciplined are you?
This affects all aspects of working at or from home. How good are you at settling down and concentrating for an extended period, or do you tend to jump from one thing to another? How good would you be not just at getting started in the morning, but remembering to take time off and STOP? Are you a latent workaholic? Could you allow the fax to run while you were having a drink with your wife or husband at the end of the day, or would you need to take a quick look? Conversely, could you leave the washing up not done or the house untidy and sit down to work without worrying? Do you tend to worry about work-related or indeed other problems, or do you find it easy to let go and switch off? Are you a compulsive snacker? If given the opportunity, would you keep eating biscuits or snacks to distract, reward, or cheer yourself up? Will you make sure that you do get out of the house if your work is predominantly done at home most of the time? Is keeping fit important to you, and something you do regularly?

How practical is it?
It may seem like a good idea, but how disruptive will it be in terms of space, relationships and day-to-day practicalities? Do you have, or can you create, the necessary space which is then not available to the rest of the family most, if not all, of the time? Has your spouse or partner traditionally stayed at home, and will he or she feel that their private space and time, over which they have previously had complete control, has been invaded with negative rather than positive side effects? Some families and relationships work well because there are distinct boundaries, and time

spent apart. Does yours? How good would you be at hearing your children crying or fighting and letting someone else, such as a spouse or childminder, take care of the problem, or enjoy the excitement if it were a happy event?

If you were thinking about combining teleworking with a move to a more rural area, could you cope with the multiple sources of stress of moving house, changing work patterns, losing friends and neighbours, and the combined effects on you and the rest of the family? Would you still be able to go to the office easily for meetings?

Chapter 7

Thriving on your own

So, you're on your own. You have decided to become a teleworker. You have answered the questions; discussed the issues posed in the last chapter with your manager and family. You are ready to start. Now you need to be able to make the most of your new-found freedom and opportunity. This is the day-to-day management from the other side of the fence.

Create a barrier

Although most of us complain about commuting, and avoiding it is often a prime reason to start teleworking, the daily commute does provide an important transition from home to work. It is a ritual or psychological switch that puts us in another gear and mode of action, and back again at the end of the day. You still need that switch. Options include going for a short walk, for example, to collect the newspaper; wearing office clothes while working; using a particular cup or mug for coffee; starting the day with the newspaper and opening post, reading messages; making out the day's to-do list. It does not matter what it is, as long as it works for you.

Establish the ground rules with family, friends and neighbours from the outset

Having clear-cut ground rules helps you, as much as it helps everyone else. This is especially important for small children who may not understand why Mummy or Daddy is here, but not here. Again there are various options including making your work room a no-go area, especially for children; set specific times for breaks at lunch time or tea time when you are there and have time to play or talk. You need to make clear at the outset that little jobs around the house cannot, and will not, be done while you are working.

Find child-care or elder-care you trust

This applies whether you work at or away from home, but is particularly important if the child- or elder-care is nearby or in the home while you are working, and the temptation is therefore greater to stay, or to check how they are.

You don't have to be alone

The phone is now not only an essential tool, but also the "coffee machine", the "chance meeting in the corridor", the "pop next door to explore an idea", the "grapevine" and a "lifeline". In other words, you must use it to keep in touch in every possible way. Use it for all the reasons that you ever talked to people in the office.

Get out of the house at least once a day

Peace and quiet can turn into a daunting silence if it goes on for too long without a break: you need to remember that the outside world is still there, and to have a bit of exercise. Go for a short walk; have lunch in a local café, restaurant or pub on a regular, but not necessarily on a daily basis – you may find someone else working from home in the process. Go to the local shops for a few small items and get to know the shopkeepers well enough for a short chat. People working from home are also beginning to set up their own networks to provide support, company and ideas. These too can provide a route out of the house.

Give yourself a complete break at lunch time

A change is as good as a rest, as the saying goes. Giving yourself a complete break and even a treat such as listening to a particular radio programme, or watching a recording of an interesting TV programme, can improve your concentration enormously in the afternoon; have a short sleep if you are really tired; take the dog for a walk; go for a swim or a jog.

Is there anybody there?

Advertise locally, join or even set up an organisation for people working from home whether in your area or elsewhere. Alternatively, find out if there are local organisations which meet during the day, or at lunchtime, which you could join.

Chapter 8

In control and in touch: managing communications

From management by osmosis to management by design

Communications are central to resolving two of the main objections to teleworking: the perceived loss of management control over employees, and the dangers of isolation for employees. Both require a shift from informal, largely ad hoc, face-to-face communication, to more formal, pre-arranged communication, much but not all of which will be remote. It is a case of making explicit that which has been implicit. Three simple guidelines will help: keep talking, keep them visible, and keep everyone informed. Both sides have a responsibility in the process, but ultimately the buck stops with the managers. It is their job to know what their employees are doing, to monitor their performance on a regular basis, specify targets and longer term objectives, and provide their longer term career development and training.

When everyone is in the same place most of the time a great deal of communication passes through the informal network, over the grapevine, via the coffee machine, by seeing the comings and goings which indicate new activity. This informal communication can compensate for considerable gaps in the formal flows of information within a department and from one department to another. When some of the people are away most of the time, the gaps and cracks appear very quickly, and can have devastating effects.

Technology has a significant role to play in easing the way, but technology alone has never been the total solution to anything. Forward planning, careful scheduling and commitments to central diaries and information are what drive the technology and ensure that all the necessary meetings are in place.

The phone as a way of life

As already mentioned in the previous chapter, regular and effective use of the phone is central to ensuring that those working at home stay in touch and involved in the department. Talking on the phone has to become as natural as chatting by the coffee machine.

Regular office days

Very few schemes actually operate on a 100 percent at-home basis. Most of them have set times of the week or amounts of time when the employee will be in the office. In most cases, days and hours to be worked at home or in the office are discussed and agreed from the outset. Ideally, they should be written into the contract.

Regular daily calls

If managers talk to their employees on a daily basis in the office, then there is no reason not to do so at least as frequently once they are remote. This need not be a particularly formal conversation – it can be equivalent to stopping by someone's desk for a chat, but a recognition that they are out there is important. Some of this can be transferred to e-mail, or fax where the communication is supplementary or involves the transfer of written information. The addition of simple, personal messages asking how the film was, or if the evening went well, or whether their child is better, show that the person, as well as the job, is not forgotten.

Core contact times

Although flexibility and personal control over their work time is a goal for many teleworkers, lack of availability is a problem for managers. E-mail and answer machines go a long way to helping resolve the problem, as a large proportion of communication is the one-way transmission of information rather than discussion, but employees still need to be accessible. In many schemes, as a result, there are core hours when people must be available.

Regular departmental/ team meetings

Loss of team identity affects both sides of the team, those still in the office and the teleworkers, and there are possible dangers of 'them and us' attitudes developing. Regular departmental or team meetings are an important factor not only in discussing the relevant work issues such as reviewing progress, assigning new tasks etc, but also in facilitating the social chit-chat that holds the group together in a less tangible way. Both are essential and both must be catered for by setting aside adequate time. This may require less formal meetings incorporating lunch, or simply adding in lunch to extend the formal aspect of the meeting to give the process time.

While specific team meetings may occur on a weekly basis, wider departmental meetings should be also scheduled at least once a month. Again, e-mail can facilitate the process by keeping the airwaves open if schedules make weekly meetings problematic.

Meeting days
Targeting one particular day of the week as the prime meeting day avoids unnecessary travel and disruption for teleworkers, especially those with long distances to travel. The possibility of ad hoc communication increases if office-based colleagues and other teleworkers all know that there is a good chance of finding people in on specific days, as do the opportunities for drinks at lunch time and other social events.

Teleworker support groups
Staying in touch with office-based colleagues left behind is a part of the issue, the other is building an *esprit de corps* among teleworkers. Providing them with their own network and opportunities to meet and discuss issues, problems and successes is central to this process. This can occur as much via e-mail as face-to-face. In fact both are necessary to maintain continuity.

Social events
Most companies have occasional social events. Where telework schemes are operating, these are essential and need to be more frequent. They provide a means to reinforce the individual's identification with their

department and the organisation; a chance to meet office-based colleagues and an opportunity to meet other teleworkers. Such events give people the chance to voice any concerns or problems they see arising or feel they have. These may be discussed in a relaxed, informal manner; or arrangements can be made for a more formal meeting to sort them out. This may help to prevent small problems developing into significant difficulties.

E-mail systems can also provide an important social outlet by using bulletin boards as the 'pub' – where people can 'meet' to chat: it provides the 'small ads' section of social events, things to sell, etc.

Staying on the circulation list
Ensuring that all teleworkers receive all the internal memos, newsletters, and general documentation about life back at the office means they know what is happening, and feel remembered. How communications are delivered is less important, post or e-mail etc, providing they arrive at their main workplace, and do not languish in a mailbox somewhere gathering dust.

The company newsletter
Incorporate a teleworkers' column into the company newsletter. It can provide news about the scheme and the participants for the wider organisation, and so keep the people involved firmly on the map. In the long term this can also act as a useful recruitment vehicle for new participants.

Telework newsletter
In addition to including news about telework in the company newsletter, a teleworkers' newsletter allows participants to share ideas and information in more detail among themselves. This again must include official and unofficial news and information, so that family events and such like get recognized.

An informed centre
Although technology can do a great deal in terms of transferring calls etc, it is still essential for someone in the office to co-ordinate teleworkers' and managers' diaries and schedules. This necessitates both technology and people, technology in the form of accessible, shared, departmental electronic diaries so that, for example, if more than one member of a team is needed for a client meeting a date can be arranged quickly and efficiently. This task often results in an enhanced role for secretarial and administrative staff in the office, who have taken on new responsibilities in managing both teleworkers' and managers' work schedules and their other commitments.

Trade union access
Trade unions should still have full access to employees, and *vice versa*, to provide additional sources of advice, representation and support. Teleworking may also of course require the trade unions to develop new ways of communicating and become *au fait* with the new technologies.

Space implications
While saving on space and overheads can be a significant benefit of teleworking to the company, teleworkers still need space in the office, albeit not as much and often of a different kind. However, this is not the case if staff have gone to a purely self-employed contractual relationship with the organisation.

More meeting rooms
Teleworkers may need less dedicated personal space, or none at all, in the office, but there is likely to be an increased demand for meeting rooms of various sizes. These, to a certain extent, will replace personal offices to enable people to talk in peace.

Dual use space
There is often space within many organisations which is underutilized, for example the canteen. Decor and furniture often preclude its use for

anything other than its prime function. Redesigning these areas can make them suitable for informal work meetings.

Quiet rooms for 'hot-desking'
Those employees working only a small part of their hours at home will still have their own desks in the office as usual. Those who spend most of their time out of the office at home or with clients still need a base in the office and somewhere they can work in peace when they are there. This needs to be sufficiently familiar to be 'personal', but not necessarily solely for the individual's own use.

The quiet rooms need to have adequate work space, dedicated filing space for individuals' own papers – possibly mobile ones which they can then bring to their work space – and dedicated terminals providing access to all the necessary in-house systems. People intending to spend time in the office can then book a space.

Helplines and support
Technical helplines for software and systems support are a common feature of life with computers. As already mentioned, corporate, or possibly external, versions of these are needed for teleworker technical support for all their equipment. But teleworkers will need more than technical assistance: the more fragile, human aspects will need support too. This support will be provided, in part, by the communications, meeting and planning procedures mentioned above.

In the early stages of a scheme's introduction, teleworkers will almost certainly need a great deal of reassurance and help with many technical and human problems, both of a trivial and a substantial nature. It is vital that they receive that help and assurance.

A central helpline
A central helpline should provide a wide-ranging service which can provide everything from a sympathetic ear to an informed and immediate

response of how to deal with a crisis when it arrives. Staff running the helpline should know where to find information or help if they do not have an immediate answer to any query or problem posed by teleworkers. Needless to say, confidentiality is essential. Helpline staff would then build up a wealth of insight and experience which would improve the service and the answers given to callers. The problems and queries dealt with by the helpline would provide an important input in the fine tuning of a teleworking scheme.

One-to-one mentors
To help new recruits to a telework scheme adapt quickly and easily, a mentor system can be used. The new teleworkers are assigned to a colleague who helps them through the initial few months. The mentor need not be a manager, but can be someone of similar status and function in the department or elsewhere in the organisation who builds a direct link back to the office. They are someone to chat to, share problems with, who will help the teleworker generally keep in touch with what's going on. This is particularly effective if people new to the organisation are teleworking from the outset, since they will not have had the opportunity to develop their own network of friends and contacts.

Counselling
Some organisations are already successfully running employee counselling programmes, and any such programme should of course be extended to teleworkers. Such a service would be confidential and staffed by trained counsellors. It would provide psychological support, help people identify if they were suffering from significant problems such as isolation, stress or depression, or simply provide skilled support to avoid such problems developing. This could be provided on a contract basis by an external counselling service.

Technology

Technology has a central role in ensuring good communications. Making the most of what technology is already available is even more important for teleworkers than elsewhere in the organisation. Chapter 9 deals with the type of equipment needed to run a telework scheme successfully, and demonstrates that it does not necessarily require particularly sophisticated systems.

Chapter 9

Assessing the home as the workplace

All companies will already be familiar with the prevailing regulations governing normal working conditions. A shift to home-based working raises many important new issues, to both employee and employer. These especially apply to implementation of those regulations, the protection of employees and their rights to privacy, defining responsibilities and clarifying procedures which recognize all these elements.

As with so many significant innovations, the main problem is that actual practice has moved ahead of the legislative framework. At the end of 1992, there was little or no legislation designed specifically for teleworking. That said, there is of course a vast array of regulations and legislation which must be taken into account. Some legislation which relates to traditional forms of homeworking adds complications, for example, the Heimarbeitsgesetz in Germany.

The legislative implications have been particularly well researched in Germany where a number of books and reports have been published itemizing the legal statutes which apply. As teleworking continues to develop and become more widespread, more specific regulations, and information on them, will appear. This is an area where trade unions are also focusing their activity.

PLEASE NOTE: The discussions in this section are intended solely as a guide to some of the issues so far encountered in various European countries. They are intended to help smooth the way to successful teleworking. They do not constitute legal advice, nor can they be regarded as finite and comprehensive, since the legislative and regulatory framework for teleworking is only now developing. Anyone setting up a telework scheme should take professional advice and consult the relevant organisations at national and local level.

The areas covered are drawn from the existing company and union agreements – especially in the UK and Germany – and from discussions with practitioners. These points must all be covered in the telework agreements so that managers and teleworking employees all know who is responsible for what and under what circumstances.

Definition of a workplace

The definition of a workplace, and whether workplace regulations apply, is central to the debate. In most instances, companies have defined the home-based workplace as an extension of the normal workplace, so that the organisation can continue to take on its statutory responsibilities within a framework of joint responsibility with the employee. The issue then at stake is how to do this while preserving the privacy and legal status of the individual's home – which in Germany, for example, is laid down in the Constitution.

This affects a number of other areas, ranging from the regulatory issues of health and safety to the practical matter of who pays the phone bill.

Health and safety

The key questions on health and safety are the observation of standards and procedures, and access for inspection and verification. Most companies require the installation of all equipment, systems and electricity supply by recommended, professionally trained staff approved by the company. These can be third party organisations which would then operate in the same way as any contractor the individual would normally allow into the home. Inspections can be conducted on the same basis, avoiding the necessity of the company having direct access to the home. Guidelines on these procedures should be incorporated in the terms and conditions.

Training also plays an important role. People in offices are often unaware of the regulations which apply, and why they were developed. Training which enables them to understand the significance of the issues, coupled with detailed checklists for people to complete, provides a sound basis on which to develop joint responsibility. Table 12 lists some key areas to cover in a self-completion home check list.

Table 12: Home checklist

Working area
- ☐ Secure, dedicated, lockable work area;
- ☐ Ease of access to workplace;
- ☐ Secure, lockable storage – desk, cupboard, filing cabinet;
- ☐ Letters sent to local authority

Security
- ☐ Burglar alarm;
- ☐ Escape in case of fire/emergency;
- ☐ Fire/smoke detector/fire extinguisher;
- ☐ Dangerous or inflammable materials, eg asbestos;
- ☐ Obstructions, eg on stairs;

Health and safety
- ☐ Electricity supply and equipment;
  - professionally installed with adequate plugs
  - circuit breakers and surge repressors where necessary
- ☐ All equipment in good working order;
- ☐ Adequate space, heating, lighting, ventilation;
- ☐ Appropriate sitting, desk and terminal arrangement;
  - screen position to avoid glare
  - relative height of desk and chair for posture, back support, and to minimize strain
- ☐ Adequate working and storage facilities and equipment;
- ☐ Emergency services informed of any mobility problem;

Insurance
- ☐ Letter to insurance company;
- ☐ Insurance organized by employer;
- ☐ Third party insurance;
- ☐ Equipment insurance;
- ☐ Any other particular concerns.

In most instances the results will provide fairly straightforward advice, consisting of a list of 'dos and don'ts'. In some cases, minor alterations such as new cabling/sockets may be needed. All costs should be covered by the company. Where major alterations are necessary to create an appropriate work space, each company must decide on the merits of the case. However, the individual would probably be considered an unsuitable candidate.

Despite the concerns about invasion of privacy, most employees are happy for their work areas to be checked: there is, after all, a significant level of self-interest in ensuring appropriate working conditions.

In many ways, the health and safety regulations relating to the equipment and work area are easier to enforce than those relating to such matters as VDU usage and the need for regular breaks: the temptation is always to continue especially if there is a deadline to meet or a target to achieve. Teleworkers need to be made aware of the importance of regular breaks and well sited and adjustable seating and equipment. Training is important to help people understand what problems may occur, for example, the dangers of Repetitive Strain Injury, and how to recognize early symptoms.

This advice and training must be further backed up by clear, easy to understand guidelines and procedures covering:

- equipment usage: who is and is not allowed to use it;
- how best to organise work to minimize any health risk – frequency of breaks, varying activities as much as possible etc;
- what to do if equipment fails;
- who is responsible for equipment repair, and how it is organised;
- how to define work-related accidents;
- what to do in the case of an accident;
- clarification of third party liability, and what is deemed to be an accident or negligence;
- extensions to any existing company insurance policies – how guidelines will be updated and employees informed of significant changes.

Existing company practice and policy will provide the foundation for issues which must be addressed, and how they will be handled. The significant difference for teleworkers is that they must be far more aware of, and able to deal with, immediate problems as they occur. However, a general rule of 'if in doubt, shout' should be accepted by employee and employer alike. A helpline set up by the company should give teleworkers access to necessary information and advice and will, hopefully, avoid unnecessary mistakes and complications. Where significant numbers of employees are teleworkers, a dedicated telework health and safety specialist adviser should ensure that the telework aspect of any new regulations are considered and incorporated into company policy as soon as possible.

Tax

Tax regulations are another area where the change of status of the home, or at least a part of it, needs to be clarified. For example, in the UK, a room solely and exclusively used for business purposes may make employees liable to pay business rates on that portion of their property. In addition, if they own the property and then sell it, they may need to pay Capital Gains Tax on a portion of the increase in value of the property. At present, the interpretation of the phrase 'solely and exclusively' has been flexible, and the problem rarely arises.

Whatever the circumstances, the company's accountants or local tax offices will be able to clarify what tax regulations apply. Employees should contact their own tax office directly: a standard draft letter provided by the company outlining the issues will ensure that they ask all the relevant questions.

Planning regulations

Planning regulations defining residential areas and the activities permitted there may present problems in some areas. Control of business use is usually an issue if it is likely to cause danger or disruption, for example, increased traffic, regular deliveries, use of noisy equipment, use of dangerous substances. Since these rarely apply to teleworking, it is not often an issue, but they will need clarification. Again, the simplest approach is to provide employees with a draft letter outlining the type of activity and amount of time involved which they can send to the appropriate authorities.

Data protection

The 1981 EC directive on data protection forms the basis of all the national legislation. Employers should already ensure they comply with the terms and conditions of registration, data storage and use.

Teleworkers will need to be familiar with the principles of the legislation and companies should confirm that all employees, wherever they work, are covered by their existing registration. If not, they will need to register in their own right.

Insurance

The use of the home as workplace may affect home insurance policies. As already indicated, it is preferable that the company pay third party liability, accident-related insurance and equipment insurance as an extension to their existing policies. It is possible that this could create a conflict with the employees' domestic insurance policies and their claims policies. Again, a standard letter sent by the employees to their insurance company informing them of the situation should suffice.

Running costs

Cutting costs and overheads is the stated aim of many schemes. As a result, unions have perceived teleworking as a deliberate means of transferring costs previously paid for by the employer to the employee. In particular, they are concerned with issues such as who pays for the extra heating, lighting and telephone costs incurred by someone working from home. Trade unions and employees may also be concerned about the loss of subsidized canteen meals, coffee and travel costs incurred by the teleworker travelling to and from the office for meetings.

- heating and lighting costs obviously do increase for the employee and, in most cases, companies provide a monthly allowance to compensate.
- in most schemes, a separate phone line for business use is installed by the company and all related installations, rental and call charges are paid for by the company. Itemized bills provide a useful back-up for monitoring calls, and for analysing costs and changes in usage resulting from teleworking.
- other expenses which may be incurred, such as photocopying, minor equipment or stationery needs, are also usually met by the company when accompanied by proof of purchase.
- travel costs to departmental meetings, training sessions etc. are mostly met by the company, since the employees are required to go from their main place of work to another location. Travel costs to client organisations are also met in the usual way.

Other issues

Tenancy agreements or mortgage terms and conditions may have exclusion clauses concerning the use of the home as a workplace. While this has seldom occurred, clarification in the form of a standard letter from the employees in question may also be necessary. Moving house suddenly takes on a new dimension – is it suitable for work? The company will need to be notified before finalizing a move in case there are wider issues or problems. The checking procedures will, of course, also have to be updated.

Chapter 10

Defining equipment needs

The growth in teleworking has paralleled and indeed been underpinned by the growth in information technology: PC's, mobile phones, e-mail, ISDN, to name but a few examples. Terms such as 'the electronic cottage' conjure up images of cosy rooms stacked full of all the latest equipment, humming productively. But how much of the technical equipment available is really necessary? It depends, just as it would depend on the job and skills of an individual in any office. The key difference is the type of communication that will be required.

Assessing needs

The analysis of individual jobs for their suitability for teleworking provides a good starting point. From this you will be able to determine such parameters as:

- whether the work will be done predominantly at home, or from home with a high mobile component involving client or customer contact;
- the range of activities to be undertaken, for example, report writing, sales analysis, data entry, software development;
- the type of information needed – central databases, external databases, project specific information;
- the level of sensitivity or confidentiality of the information;
- the frequency and type of access needed – occasional but immediate, daily and constant, daily and immediate but only for short time periods;
- the amounts and type of data to be transferred;
- high/low telephone usage.

Where to go for help

Having established what information and communication needs individual teleworkers are likely to have, the next task is to find out about the full range of systems and services available which might make everyone's lives easier. There are a number of potential sources of advice:

- ❐ The company's own systems/IT department: while their expertise may be focused on internal, conventional office needs, they will know about developments and understand the terminology;
- ❐ the PTTs and telecoms equipment suppliers, many of which now have teleworking schemes as well as advisory and consulting services;
- ❐ the computer companies – especially those already operating schemes. Many of these also provide advice and consultancy;
- ❐ specialist telework consultants;
- ❐ conventional systems consultants.

What people have

As already indicated, a telework system does not necessarily need a vast array of highly sophisticated equipment. What it does need is appropriate and regular use of the equipment that is there, especially the phone. Equipment in the home usually includes most of the following:

- ❐ separate phone line and phone for business use with a range of programmable and storage features, paid for by the company;
- ❐ PC, printer and a full range of software or, if data entry is the main task, a basic terminal;
- ❐ answerphone – not just to ensure that calls can be returned, but to give teleworkers control over the times when they are available;
- ❐ fax, not just for its use as a means of transmitting information, but to provide a basic photocopier if the need for one is low;
- ❐ modem to provide access to e-mail and the wide range of systems and services available. Relatively few schemes actually make use of modems for file transfer, although they are increasing for e-mail connection.

Additional equipment for those who are mobile and work from, rather than at, home may include:

- pager
- mobile phone
- portable PC with an internal modem.

The external systems and services which people use include:

- the post – some schemes rely exclusively on the traditional postal system for the exchange of information, sending discs and hard copy back and forth as necessary;

- courier services – for emergencies;

- e-mail provides a vital link not only back to the organisation but between all the teleworkers themselves. The existence and use of e-mail within an organisation is often a good cultural indicator of the potential to adapt to telework. However, it is still relatively infrequent outside the IT/computer company schemes;

- voice-mail – the equivalent of a systems based answerphone which, as with e-mail, is readily accessible wherever the individual user is, as long as a modem is available;

- automatic call back facilities, for example for direct access to company computers, to ensure not only that the company pays for the call but an extra layer of security, since only a restricted set of call back numbers would be recognized;

- tied lines or leased lines. These are usually only viable if there is very heavy data traffic between two locations, such as the main office and a neighbourhood office or satellite office;

- public data networks to provide access to the full range of information and data services now available.

With the upgrading of the telecoms network, the spread of ISDN and growing competition in the telecoms business, the range of more sophisticated options available via the normal phone system is growing.

This includes new services such as:

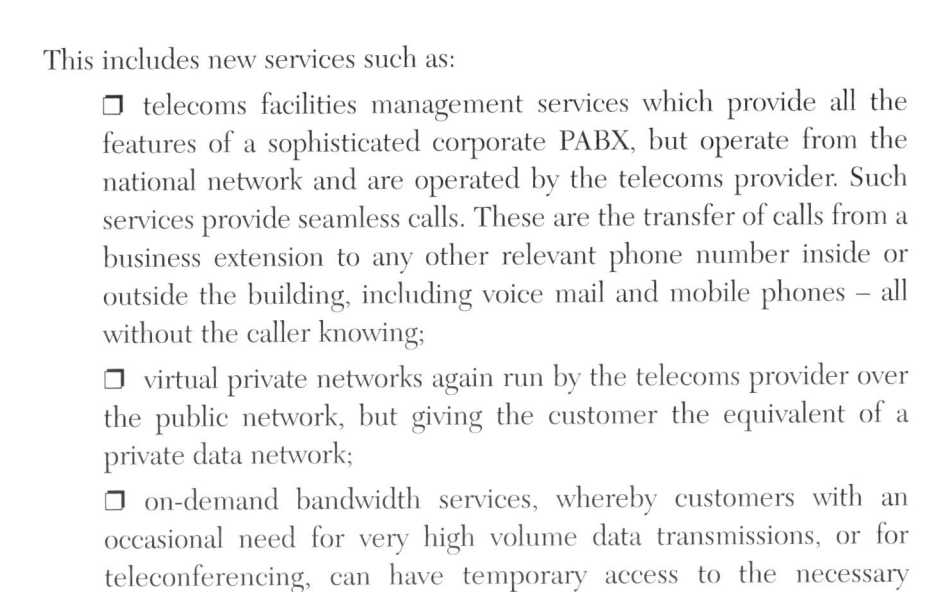

- telecoms facilities management services which provide all the features of a sophisticated corporate PABX, but operate from the national network and are operated by the telecoms provider. Such services provide seamless calls. These are the transfer of calls from a business extension to any other relevant phone number inside or outside the building, including voice mail and mobile phones – all without the caller knowing;
- virtual private networks again run by the telecoms provider over the public network, but giving the customer the equivalent of a private data network;
- on-demand bandwidth services, whereby customers with an occasional need for very high volume data transmissions, or for teleconferencing, can have temporary access to the necessary bandwidth.

Costs

Given the wide variety of options available it is almost impossible to put an average cost on setting up a teleworker. It has been done for as little as under £1000 by a local authority in the UK which was able to find second-hand reconditioned terminals adequate to their needs for part time data entry. On the other hand, a single computer system can cost upwards of £10,000 if a complex graphics system will be needed.

Whatever the costs, the company should pay the bill for supply, maintenance, running costs and support.

Technical support

Technical support is vital. In the office there is usually someone who takes on the role of unofficial departmental computer specialist and who knows how to get the best out of the software. They enjoy finding out about systems and passing on the information. Failing that, there are always other users to whom you can turn for suggestions. When a telework scheme is introduced, this informal support needs to be replaced with friendly, easily accessible technical support including manuals, personalised user guides, personal streamlined logon procedures, help lines, training sessions and maintenance expertise.

The informal support may still be there and indeed may grow among the teleworkers, since they will all be facing similar problems. The difficulty, if you are not an expert, is that you are not able to see the screen nor experiment directly on the system and watch the result. It needs experts on a par with the software support helplines provided by the software companies.

Technology has a significant role to play – the concept is after all TELEworking, but as yet the telecoms input remains relatively low and the potential underutilized. While this is often because POTS (the plain old telephone service) is adequate to the task, and simplicity is often the best policy, making the most of what is already there can make life a lot easier. However, keeping up with the technical developments may enable you to provide new impetus to your telework scheme.

Data Security

Some companies have very tight restrictions on the type of information which is allowed out of the main office. Often no confidential information about employees is allowed into teleworkers' homes in case the backs of discarded photocopies get used for painting and drawing, or someone simply decides to be nosey, or any of the other one hundred and one accidents waiting to happen occurs and the information falls into the wrong hands.

Data security in its wider context is a major concern, although ultimately if a hacker wants to get into a system, he or she will – wherever the system. That said, an assessment of the security needs and the level of sophistication required must be an integral part of the equipment supply process. All the usual forms of security will need to be instigated but may well need to be enhanced with additional data encryption techniques if sensitive information is being transferred on a regular basis. As encryption techniques improve, so the security of remote sites – of all kinds – will be less problematic.

Again, existing practices within the organisation are the prime starting point. Not everyone who uses a PC is necessarily the one who does the PC housekeeping – regular back ups, locking away copies of data, archiving and so on. As a result, training and guidelines should start from absolute basics. To emphasize the potential disaster of losing information or data through careless archiving or storage of electronic data, people should be made to think through how, if at all, they could restore a nearly completed report or replicate a complicated series of analyses. Guidance and training to help them learn the basics of good data storage and retrieval should be integral part of the teleworking scheme.

Chapter 11

Terms and conditions
– a summary

Most of the points listed below have been referred to in the text already. They have been drawn from an amalgam of sample company agreements in the USA, UK, and Germany; trade union recommendations especially in the UK and Germany; consulting and research organisation recommendations.

- Participation must be voluntary with all parties directly involved in agreement – the final decision must rest with the immediate manager or supervisor.

- Participants should retain full employee status.

- Pay and conditions should not be altered to the detriment of the employee.

- Employees should have full statutory rights with regard to unemployment benefit, sick leave entitlement, maternity leave entitlement, and a period of notice in the case of dismissal.

- Hours of work and the scheduling of those hours across the week should be agreed in advance. Overtime should be agreed on a regular basis.

- Employees should keep and regularly present records of the hours worked.

- The teleworking agreement can be terminated on either side and a job with similar pay and responsibilities should be found for the employee within the office.

- Teleworkers should be informed about, and be eligible to apply for, any appropriate job opportunities and vacancies which are available in the organisation.

- Regular performance assessments will be given, as will recommendations for any training which is appropriate.

- The company shall provide appropriate and well-maintained equipment for the use of the teleworker for the duration of their time as a teleworker.

- ❐ The company will pay for installation, supply, maintenance and insurance of the equipment.
- ❐ All equipment shall be returned to the organisation if the employee leaves the organisation, or ceases to work from home.
- ❐ Health and safety standards will apply in the workplace, and will be checked regularly. Reasonable access to the home-based workplace must be guaranteed in the interests of all parties.
- ❐ The company will provide all the necessary third party liability, and accident related insurance.
- ❐ Employee travel costs incurred in the course of work will be reimbursed by the company in full.
- ❐ The company will pay the extra home costs such as heating, lighting and telephone bills arising as a consequence of telework.
- ❐ The employee is responsible for ensuring adequate child- or elder-care.
- ❐ Employees will have access to trade union representation and be able to attend meetings within work hours. Trade unions will also have access to teleworkers.
- ❐ Appropriate training will be provided, and teleworkers will be eligible for any other training opportunities on offer within the company.
- ❐ Employees will notify employers if they intend to move house.

Appendices

Appendix 1
Useful contact addresses — 94

Appendix 2
Selected bibliography — 101

Appendix 3
Evaluation questionnaires for participants and their managers — 108

APPENDIX 1 – USEFUL CONTACT ADDRESSES

UK

Trade Union Congress (TUC)
Congress House
23-28 Great Russell Street
London WC1B 3LS
Tel: (071) 636 4030

The Institute of Management
2 Savoy Court
London WC2R 0EZ
Tel: (071) 497 0580

Data Protection Registrar
Springfield House
Water Lane
Wilmslow
Cheshire SK9 5AX
Tel: (0625) 535777

Health and Safety Executive
Broad Lane
Sheffield S3 7HQ
Tel: (0742) 892 000

IT Safety Committee Electronic and Business Equipment Association (EEA)
Russell Square House
10-12 Russell Square
London WC1B 5AE
Tel: (071) 437 0678

Organisations offering research and consultancy services in telework

Association of Rural Community Councils in England (ACRE)
Somerford Court
Somerford Road
Cirencester
Gloucestershire GL7 1TW
Tel: (0285) 653 477

Beacon Group
11 Jew Street
Brighton
East Sussex BN1 1UT
Tel: (0273) 26579

British Telecommunications plc
Teleworking Marketing Manager
81 Newgate Street
London EC1A 7AJ
Tel: (0800) 800 854

Francis Kinsman and his Associates
4 Sion Hill Place
Bath
Avon
Tel: (0225) 331807

Henley Work Forum
c/o Henley Research Centre
Greenlands
Henley-on-Thames
Oxon RG9 3AU
Tel: (0491) 571 454

IT World
18 Buckingham Gate
London SW1E 6LB
Tel: (071) 828 7300

Mercury Communications Limited
New Mercury House
26 Red Lion Square
London WC1R 4HQ
Tel: (0500) 500 194

National Association of Teleworkers
The Island House
Midsomer Norton
Bath
Avon BA3 2HL
Tel: (0761) 413 869

Solon Consultants
25 Bedford Row
London WC1R 4HE
Tel: (071) 242 2261

The Flexible Work Company
43 Water Lane
Chelveston
Wellingborough
Northants NN9 6AF
Tel: (0933) 460 951

The Home Office Partnership
The Jeffreys Building
St Johns Innovation Park
Cambridge CB4 4WS
Tel: (0223) 421 911

EU organisations

Direction F, DG XIII
European Commission
200, rue de la Loi
B-1049 Bruxelles
Belgium

European Telework Forum (set up by DG XIII)
c/o Protocol Communications Ltd
1A Castle Street
Totnes
Devon TQ9 5NU
U.K.
Tel: (0803) 865 852

BELGIUM

Association nationale pour la prévention des accidents du travail
(Health and safety information)
Rue Gachard 88
Boîte 4
B-1050 Bruxelles
Tel: (32) 26 48 03 37

Commission de la Protection de la vie Privée
Place Poelaert 3
B-1000 Bruxelles
Tel: (32) 504 66 20

FGTB (TUC Association)
Rue Haute 42 -
B-1000 Bruxelles
Tel: (32) 25 06 82 11

DENMARK

Arbejdstilsynet Direktoratet
(Health and safety information)
Landskronagade 33-35
DK-2100 Copenhagen 0
Tel: (45) 31 18 00 88

Registertilsynet
(Data protection)
Christians Brygge 284
DK-1559 Copenhagen V
Tel: (45) 33 14 38 44

Danish Employers Union (DA)
Vester Vold Gade
Postbox 112
DK-1790 Copenhagen
Tel: (45) 33 93 40 00

**LO i Denmarket
(TUC Association)**
Rosenorns Alle 21
DK-1634 Copenhagen
Tel: (45) 35 35 35 41

Odense University
Campusvej 55
DK-5230 Odense M
Tel: (45) 66 15 86 00

TFO, Teleselkabernes Forhandlingsorganisation
(Employers Association for the Telecommunications Sector)
Norregade 21
DK-1199 Copenhagen
Tel: (45) 33 99 48 40

FINLAND

Ministry of Labour
Fabianinkatu 32
PO Box 524
FIN-00101 Helsinki
Tel: (358) 0 18 56 1

Työterveyslaitos
Institute of Occupational Health
Topeliuksenkatu 41 a A
FIN-00250 Helsinki
Tel: (358) 04 74 73 83

TVK
Asemamiehenkatur 4
FIN-00520 Helsinki
Tel: (358) 01 55 1

FRANCE

Confédération Française Démocratique du Travail (CFDT)
4 Boulevard de la Villette
F-75955 Paris
Cedex 19
Tel: (33) 1 42 03 80 00

**CSC-OCDE
(TUC Association)**
26 Avenue de la Grand Armee
F-75017 Paris
Tel: (33) 1 47 63 42 63

Conseil Régional d'île de France
CATRAL (Committee Pour L'Amènagement Des Temps de

Travail et de Loisirs
Dans la Région d'île de France)
16 Boulevard Raspail
F-75007 Paris
Tel: (33) 1 40 43 84 88/89

DATAR Teletravail
Secretariat d'État a
L'Amènagement du Territoire
1 avenue Charles Fouquet
F-75343 Paris
CEDEX 07
Tel: (33) 1 40 65 12 34

Institut National de Recherche et de Sécurité
(Health and safety information)
Service CIS
30 rue Olivier-Noyer
F-75680 Paris
CEDEX 14
Tel: (33) 1 40 44 30 00

Commission Nationale de l'Informatique et des Libertés
21, rue Saint Guillaume
F-75007 Paris
Tel: (33) 1 45 44 40 65

GERMANY

B. Bit Consult
Gesellschaft für Management und Technologieberatung GmbH
Schwanthalerstraße 2
D-80336 München
Tel: (49) 89 55 58 81-3

Bundesanstalt für Arbeitsschutz
(Health and safety information)
CIS-Abteilung
Postfach 17 02 02
Vogelpothsweg 50-52
D-44149 Dortmund
Tel: (49) 23 11 76 33 41

Bundesbeauftragte für den Datenschutz
(Data protection)
Stephan-Lochner-Straße 2
Postfach 200112
D-53175 Bonn
Tel: (49) 22 88 19 95 10

Deutscher Gewerkschaftsbund Bundesvorstand (DGB)
(TUC Association)
Hans-Böckler-Straße 39
D-40476 Düsseldorf
Tel: (49) 211 43 01

Empirica
Oxfordstraße 2
D-5311 Bonn
Tel: (49) 22 89 85 30

Integrata
Biesingerstraße 10
D-72070 Tübingen
Tel: (49) 701 71/243 88

GREECE

Ministry of Labour
Centre for Occupational Health and Safety (KYAE)
6 Dodekanissou Street
GR-174 56 ALIMOS
Tel: (30) 19 91 95 66

GGCL (TUC Association)
Rue 28 October 69
GR-Athens
Tel: (30) 18 83 46 11

IRELAND

ICTU (Irish Congress of Trade Unions)
19 Raglan Road
Ballsbridge
Dublin 4
Tel: (3531) 66 80 641

National Irish Safety Organisation
CIS Unit
10 Hogan Place
Dublin 2
Tel: (3531) 66 20 39 9

Data Protection Commissioner
Department of Justice
Block 4, Irish Life Centre
Talbot Street
Dublin 1
Tel: (3531) 87 4854 4

ITALY

Confederazione Italiana Sindacati Lavoratori (CISL) (TUC Association)
Via Po 21
I-00198 Rome
Tel: (39) 68 47 31

Istituto superiore per la prevenzione e la Sicurezza del Lavoro (ISPESL)
Servizio Documentazione e Informazione
(Health and safety information)
Via Alessandria 220/e
I-00198 Rome
Tel: (39) 68 84 06 03

LUXEMBOURG

Fédération des Industriels Luxembourgeois (FEDIL) (TUC Association)
7 Rue A De Gasperi
P O Box 1304
L-1013 Luxembourg
Tel: (352) 43 53 66

Président de la Commission à la Protection des Données Nominatives
Ministère de la Justice
15 Boulevard Royal
L-2934 Luxembourg
Tel: (352) 47 94 42 3

APPENDIX 1

Telemarketing
19 Rue de Wormeldange
L-Luxembourg 6180
Gonderange
Tel: (352) 27 86 34

NETHERLANDS

Ministry of Social Affairs and Employment
(Health and safety information)
CIS Department, Library and Document Centre
P O Box 90801
NL-2509 The Hague
Tel: (31) 70 33 34 57 5

Voorzitter Registratiekamer
(Data protection registrar)
Sir Winston Churchillaan 362
Postbus 3011
NL-2280 GA

FNV
Naritaweg 10
Postbus 8456
NL-1005 Amsterdam
Tel: (31) 20 58 16 30 0

PORTUGAL

Confederação da Industria Portuguesa
(The Confederation of Portuguese Industry)
Avenue 5 de Outubro 35-1
P-1000 Lisbon
Tel: (351) 54 74 54

Confederação Geral dos Trabalhadores Portugueses – Intersindical Nacional
(TUC Association)
Rue Victor Cordon 1-3
P-1200 Lisbon
Tel: (351) 34 72 18 1

Direcção-Geral de Higien e Segurança do Trabalho
Ministério do Emprego e da Segurança Social
(Health and safety information)
Av Da República 84-5
P-1600 Lisbon
Tel: (351) 77 30 32/3/4

SPAIN

Instituto Nacional de Medicina y Seguridad de Trabajo
(Health and safety information)
Servico CIS
Cidudad Universitaria
Pabellón 8
ES-28040 Madrid
Tel: (34) 54 41 40 0

UGT-E
Hortaleza 88
ES-28004 Madrid
Tel: (34) 15 89 76 94

SWITZERLAND

Caisse Nationale Suisse d'Assurance en cas d'Accidents

Division de la prévention des accidents (Health and safety information)
Case postale 4358
Fluhmattstrasse 1
CH-6002 Lucerne
Tel: (41) 41 21 51 11

SGB (TUC Association)
Monbijoustrasse 61
Postfach 64
CH-3000 Bern 23
Tel: (41) 31 45 56 66

OTHER ORGANISATIONS

County of Los Angeles
Chief Administrative Office
Policy and Support Division
222 North Grand Avenue,
Room 585
Los Angeles
CA 90012
USA
Tel: (1) 21 39 74 26 32/37

Gil Gordon Associates
10 Donner Court
Monmouth Junction
NJ 08852
USA
Tel: (1) 20 13 29 22 66

Orange County Transportation Authority
Planning Department
11222 Acacia Parkway
Garden Grove
CA 92642
USA
Tel: (1) 71 46 38 90 00

US Telecommuting Advisory Council
1452 Edinger # 1320
Tustin
CA 92680
USA
Tel: (1) 71 42 59 65 09

APPENDIX 2 – SELECTED BIBLIOGRAPHY

The bibliography contains almost exclusively books and reports. These provide a practical introduction and overview of teleworking. Many of them also include extensive bibliographies of additional material. There are also many hundreds of newspaper and journal articles too numerous to list in full, but details of which will be accessible via any of the online databases operating in your country.

The bibliography is organised by language and then alphabetically by author/publishing organisation where appropriate.

In English

Banking, Insurance and Finance Union (BIFU): Homeworking, the potential applications and its possible consequences for BIFU; BIFU, 1990
   Union concerns in relation to the development of teleworking.

Beacon Group, The: Teleworking 92, Conference papers
   12 papers on the development of telework, management, technology and business issues.

Bibby, A: Home is where the Office is. Hodder & Stoughton
   An easy-to-read personal perspective on deciding to work from home.

Brain, D and Page, A: Review of current experiences and prospects for teleworking, 1991
   European Commission report reviewing teleworking in North America and Europe plus case studies and technological advances and products.

British Telecommunications plc: Teleworking Pack, 1992
   The economics of teleworking
   A study of the environmental impact of teleworking
   Disability and teleworking

An overview of teleworking
Clerical teleworking – how it affects family life
Teleworking: Evolution or revolution
Teleworking: Products and services
Tomorrow's workplace: The manager's guide to teleworking.

Burch, S, Teleworking: a strategic guide for management, Kogan, Page, 1991
Practical guide to the issues and development of telework from a company perspective.

Civil and Public Services Association (CSPA)/UK Treasury Guidelines for Homeworking, 1991
Outline of terms and conditions.

European Telework Forum, The: Management Issues in Telework and Mobile Working, Conference papers, 1992
Case studies from European organisations with teleworking schemes, plus papers on technological developments for mobile working.

Health and Safety Executive: Display Screen Equipment Work: Guidance on Regulations, 1992
Explanation and guide to the implications of new EU regulations.

Huws, U; Korte, W B; Robinson, S: Telework, Towards the Elusive Office. John Wiley & Sons, 1990
A review of the pros, cons and issues related to telework, plus the results of a four country survey on the extent of and interest in telework.

Insitute of Manpower Studies: Teleworking Flexibility for a few; Wilson, A; Report No 210, 1991
Six case studies reflecting current practice and the impact of teleworking on operational, managerial and employment issues.

Institute of Personnel Management: Telework: The Human Resource Implications.

Joeman, L: Department of Employment, Telework in Britain, April 1992
Reviews current status of teleworking in Britain and considers factors which underlie its expansion.

Kinsman, F: The telecommuters, John Wiley & Sons, 1987
Detailed case studies of early teleworking schemes in the UK.

Mercury Communications Limited: The telework portfolio – for large organisations.
The guidebook
Open your organisation to a new way of working (new edition pending).

Ministry of Labour of Finland, The: The P&T of Finland, The Finnish State Computer Centre, Helsinki, January 1991
Introducing flexiwork and telework in Finland
Finland: Finnish firms in the information technology industry
Finland: History of telework.

Moorcroft, S: European teleworking: A cost-effective work option for the 1990's, SRI International – Business Intelligence Program, 1991
Discusses the economic and social benefits that telework offers to employees and employers.

Murphy, E: Flexible work: Union attitudes in France, Germany and the UK; Home Office Partnership, to be published 1993
Will review trade union attitudes and developments in contractual arrangements and employment relations concerning flexible working.

National Council for Educational Technology (NCET): Training for teleworking, 1992
Outlines a training programme for teleworkers and their managers.

National Rehabilitation Board: Teleworking applications and potential (TEAPOT), 1989 Final report
Assessment of telework and its potential to provide work for the disabled.

O T R Ltd: Teleworking – what is controlling its acceptance, what are the benefits, and how should it be managed? London, 1991
Survey of senior managers, concerns re introduction of telework.

Orange County Transport Department (O C T D): Introduction to telecommuting, 1989
A practical guide to teleworking.

Society of Telecom Executives (STE), Beverley MacGowan, Guidelines for managers and teleworkers
Outline agreement, terms and conditions for the introduction of telework.

Solon Consultants: Distance working: The prospects for telework, 1992
Reviews telework literature. Research was conducted with some of the UK's largest companies to explore senior executives' attitudes towards telework.

French

Duport, J-P: Les teleservices et le telependulaire, DATAR, 1992

DATAR: L'evaluation de l'appel à projets lancé par la DATAR en 1990, 1991.

Danish

Jacobsen, A F B: Distancearbejda Fup eller fakta? HK's Arbejdsmiljoafdeling.

German

Goldmann, M; Richter, G: Teleheimarbeit von Frauen;
Betriebliche Flexibilisierungsstrategien und das Interesse von Frauen an der Vereinbarkeit von Beruf und Familie, Kurzfassung des Forschungsberichts des Landesinstitutes Sozialforschungsstelle Dortmund, 1987
> Short summary and detailed report on issues facing women combining home and work.

Heilmann, Dr W: Teleprogrammierung: Die Organisation der dezentralen Software-Produktion, Fortel Verlag Wiesbaden, 1987
> Results of a detailed research programme into the design, development and assessment of teleworking in software production by Integrata.

Kilian, W; Borsum, W; Hoffmeister, U: Telearbeit und Arbeitsrecht; Bundersministerium für Arbeit und Sozialordnung, Institut für Rechtsinformatik (IRI), Universitat Hannover, 1986.

Kreibich, R; Druke, H; Dunkelmann, H; Feuerstein, G: Zukunft der Telearbeit; Empirische Untersuchung zur Dezentralisierung und Flexibilisierung von Angestelltentätigkeiten mit Hilfe neuer Informations-und Kommunikationstechnologien, RKW-Verlag, 1990.

Lindena, B: Telearbeit; Ein Beitrag zur Diskussion über die Dezentralisierung von Angestelltentätigkeiten aufgrund moderner Informations-und Kommunikationstechniken unter besonderer Berücksichtigung bisher vorliegender Untersuchungen, 1989.

Telearbeit – elektronische Einsiedelei oder neue Form der persönlichen Entfaltung; Deutscher Gewerkschaftsbund, Düsseldorf, 1988
> Selection of papers on technical, legal and social aspects of teleworking.

Wedde, P: Telearbeit und Arbeitsrecht; Schutz der Beschäftigten und Handlungsmöglichkeiten des Betriebrates, Bund-Verlag Kohn, 1986
Teleworking and labour law in Germany, currently being updated for second edition.

Italian

Roveda, C; Campoldall'Orto, S; Cassinari, L: Telelavoro in Italia – alcuni casi
Brief review of six telework schemes in Italy.

Assosiazione Italiana Di Diritto Del Lavoro E Della Sicurezza Sociale: Il Tempo di Lavoro; Atti Delle Giornate Di Studio Di Diritto Del Lavoro, 1987

Angeli, F (Editor): Libro, contenente gli atti del Convegno organiszato del CEIL avente per tela 'Telelavoro: i miti e le prospettive concrete per l'Italia', 1984.

Paolucci, S: Il telelavoro nell banche in Italia e all'estero, l'Impressa' No 1, 1988.

Special teleworking publication of 'Industria e sindacato' No 23-24, del 21 giugno 1991

> Martino, De V; Wirth, L: Telelavoro: un nuovo modo di vivere e di lavorare
>
> Paoletti, A; Crimersmois, L: Il telelavoro nella produzione del software
>
> Bosco, E: Il telelavoro e il caso SIP-Torino
>
> Bianco, M-L: Tra necessita e scelta, atteggiamenti nei confronti del telelavoro

Testo dell'intervento di Lorenza Gaeta avente per oggetto

'Il tempo nel telelavoro' effettuato nelle giornate di studio tenutesi a Genovail il 4 – 5 aprile 1986, pubblicato nell'Annuario di Diritto del Lavoro No 20 1987.

Pan-European publications

European Foundation for the Improvement of Living and Working Conditions: Labour law and social security aspects in the EC, 1988
Review of the disparity between changing work practices and the conventional basis and form of labour law in Europe.

International Labour Office: Conditions of Work Digest, Telework Vol 9, No 1 1990.

International Labour Office: More found to work at home, A Council of Europe study, 1990.

APPENDIX 3 – EVALUATION QUESTIONNAIRES FOR PARTICIPANTS AND THEIR MANAGERS

These are examples of the type of questionnaires which can be administered before, during and after the pilot scheme to assess participants' expectations and perceptions versus the reality of teleworking. They cover practical matters such as communication with managers and colleagues, work scheduling, extra costs and problems with technology; as well as intangible aspects of how it felt.

The lists of questions given here are, however, only guidelines, and they will need adapting.

Travel information

Questions covering information about participants' commute to work – distance, type of transport used, time taken, problems encountered, etc.

Assessment of teleworking versus working in the office

Questions in this section ask participants to assess purely subjectively – with no right or wrong answers – what they think the effect of teleworking will have on aspects of their work. In response to statements on each of the following areas they must choose whether they think expectations will be higher/lower, more/less or about the same. Their early responses can then be compared with their answers to the same questions, once they have begun teleworking. In this way, people's expectations and perceptions of telework can be measured and compared with the reality.

Points to cover include:

Manager's expectations of teleworkers' work

Manager's perceptions of teleworkers' productivity

Belief that developing adequate communications with manager will be problematic

Manager's awareness of work being carried out

How, and in what form, teleworkers will receive feedback

The level of distraction at home versus the office
Level of productivity at home versus the office
The amount of flexibility over work at home versus the office
Ability to schedule time/tasks
Likelihood of working longer hours at home

Motivation to work hard
Autonomy over work load and assignments
Ability to work when it suits them

Difficulty in getting into 'work mode' or the right frame of mind
Level of professionalism, feeling or acting professionally
Feeling comfortable working at home versus working in the office
Happy that judgements about their work will be based on merit not on time spent in the office
Amount of quality time with the family

Employees working at home will be a competitive advantage for the company
Costs to the company
Costs to the employee
Overall benefits to the employee
Overall benefits to the company

Amount of manager's time needed to manage a 'remote' workforce
Scheduling meetings at short notice will be problematic

A set of statements illustrating the following points to which they can agree or disagree:

> That social isolation will be a problem
>
> That lack of professional contact will be a problem
>
> Lack of visibility in the office could impair promotion prospects
>
> Supervisor is nervous about employees being out of sight
>
> Will lose sense of identity with the company
>
> Lack of support services will be problematic
>
> They work well on their own
>
> Training has prepared them well for the realities of teleworking
>
> Their family will find it difficult to adjust to them being 'at home', but not at home
>
> Their family are supportive of them working at home
>
> Family and friends will tease them when they work at home
>
> The pressure of having to keep quiet will put a strain on their family
>
> Commuting has always been a problem
>
> Use commute time constructively
>
> Commute time is an important transition from home to work and back again

The final section should include questions dealing with the following:

> Age, sex, education, experience, previous jobs, etc
>
> Detailed information about the equipment installed, costs of setting up teleworkers, etc.

APPENDIX 3

Discussion groups

Discussion groups with participants and their managers can also cover a range of subjects. These can be run as mixed or separate groups. Responses from non-participants' and participants' departments are also useful to compare and assess the wider impact of teleworking; and the feelings and issues it is raising in the organisation.

Topics for discussion should include:

How the practicalities of the policies, guidelines and procedures are working out in reality?

How much time are teleworkers spending at home? Is it more or less than expected? Why?

Any particular responses – positive or negative – that teleworkers have had from non-teleworkers, colleagues or otherwise?

Have teleworkers found scheduling meetings and contacting people a problem?

Has management style changed, if so how and what has been good/bad?

Levels of support and help – is there enough, what is missing – for technical issues, management and administration matters?

Costs and reimbursements – have they been more/less, are the allowances enough? Anything teleworkers, their colleagues or their managers would recommend to do differently, or that should definitely be kept.

Final questionnaire

A final questionnaire could follow up on any of the issues raised in more detail with individual participants. This is to identify whether all teleworkers had similar experiences or whether some of the problems/advantages were isolated incidents.

The questionnaire covers points such as:

Time spent teleworking – more/less; reasons for difference from expectations

    eg. equipment not there

    information not there

    meetings

    team interaction too difficult

    enjoyed it and found it made a huge difference

    supervisors not supportive

    too quiet

    not enough of the right sort of work

    difficult to switch off from work

Whether teleworkers have had any specific problems with:

    overall costs – what in particular

    time management

    technical support/using the systems

    consultation with peers and colleagues

    weight gain

    ability to learn new skills

    forgetting things needed which are left at the office/home

    interruptions

    working longer

    feeling lonely

    getting started in the morning

What have been the benefits for the teleworker?
- more time for self and family
- less stressed, more relaxed to be with
- better work
- more work done in the time
- new friends and interests
- saved money on commute

Other questions to ask include:
- What could the company do to improve the project?
- What could the company do to provide more support?
- What tips would they pass on to new teleworkers?
- What tips would they pass on to new teleworker managers?
- How have they managed their work schedule?
- Has their job description changed?
- Have their colleagues' attitudes changed?
- Would they like to continue teleworking?
- Would they recommend teleworking?

Evaluation of the telework scheme is vital, if it is to succeed. By being able to analyse what makes telework succeed or fail, the organisation should be able to adjust the scheme, introduce new procedures etc. to ensure that the scheme is successful. The major elements which influence the success or otherwise of a teleworking scheme are: the people – both teleworkers and their managers; the work and the support structure – in terms of technical, managerial and administrative help.

Diaries

As well as using questionnaires and group discussions to evaluate the telework scheme, many companies are also using individual teleworker diaries to continuously monitor and analyse their progress and suitability for being teleworkers.

Management of time, and control over work are the two most important issues that need addressing to reassure managers that work is being done efficiently and satisfactorily by teleworkers. Teleworkers also need to help organise their time and schedule tasks. The diaries are used instead of standard work or time sheets for project allocation. These may be a combination of a to-do list, time log, activity log, task and appointments diary.

They are also designed to monitor the teleworker's well-being by identifying early symptoms of stress and/or isolation before they reach severe levels, as well as assessing the teleworkers' productivity and efficiency. Difficulties encountered with equipment, work, the family, etc. are recorded in the diary by teleworkers. They are then presented and discussed with the employee's manager on a monthly basis.

The diaries should also include other events that teleworkers take part in – ie. home-related or office-related activities such as visits made to the office, visits to clients, contact with other teleworkers; whether or not they belong to local telework associations, etc.

Steps taken to remain in touch with the outside world

Part of the evaluation process, for both costs and training input, should include the ways teleworkers use the communications system available to them to overcome the potential problems of isolation. Points to cover include:

Detailed logs of time spent working (recorded in the diary);

Calls made (not as part of normal office work);

Time spent at the home-desk versus time spent out and about with clients etc;

How many meetings they attend in the office and with whom;

What systems they use and how often;

How much time they work;

The breaks taken.

The company must keep track of any technical problems encountered by teleworkers and how they were dealt with. Where did they go for help? Did they use informal help from a colleague, or formal help? Did they solve the problem? How long did it take?

INDEX

A
absenteeism, 24
accounts, 49
addresses, 94-100
administrative staff, 68
agreements, 52, 74-5
   termination of, 90
answer machines, 65, 83

B
back offices, 14
bandwidth services, 85
barriers, 60
benefits, table of, 24
bibliography, 101-6
break-times, 61
business exchanges, 14

C
career development, 53
Caribbean, the, 14
CD Roms, 20
child-care, 27, 50, 60, 91
circulation list, 67
cities, 18, 19, 24
clerical work, 45
communication
   informal, 64
communication skills, 36
communications
   management of, 64-71
communities, regeneration of, 24
community telework centres, 14

commuting
   avoidance of, 14, 22, 24
   problems of, 23
   psychological switch, 60
company identity, 27
competitiveness, 18
computers, 19, 83
   data storage and retrieval, 87
   health and safety
     regulations, 77
   portable, 20
   role of, 17
conditions of employment, 52, 90
confidentiality, 27, 86-7
contact times, 65
contracts, 36
   short-term, 53
core contact times, 65
corporate issues, 17-8
corporate teleworking, 15
cost cutting, 18, 26, 52
costs
   detailed records, 37
   of equipment, 85
   responsibility for, 79-80
   set-up costs, 91
   of teleworking, 27-28
counselling, 70
couriers, 84
customer satisfaction, 49, 51

D
data entry, 49
data protection, 79, 86-7
deadlines, 49-50
departmental meetings, 65-6

Deutscher Gewerkschatsbund, 29
Digital, 26-7
disabled employees, 19, 24
dismissal, 53
  notice of, 90
dual use space, 68-9

E
e-mail, 20, 65, 66, 83
  bulletin boards, 67
  role of, 84
economic issues, 17-8
elder-care, 27, 60, 91
Empirica, 17
employees. *see also* selection criteria
  advantages for, 25-6
  disadvantages for, 27-9
  opposition to teleworking, 16
  selection of, 40-2
  status of, 27, 52-3, 90
  successful teleworking, 60-1
  suitability for teleworking, 56-8
employers
  advantages for, 26-7
  disadvantages for, 27-9
encryption, 87
environmental issues, 19, 24
equal pay, 53
equipment
  assessing needs, 82
  help with, 82-3
  installation of, 36, 75
  responsibility for, 33, 90-1
  running costs, 79-80
  technical helplines, 69-70

technical support, 85-6
training in, 36
types available, 83-5
escape route, 37
European Commission, 19
European Union
  environmental concerns, 19
  skills shortages, 17
  teleworking in, 13
evaluation, 43. *see also* questionnaires
  of pilot scheme, 36-7
exploitation, 28, 49

F
facsimile machines, 20, 65, 83
families
  and teleworking, 57-8, 60
feasibility study, 32
fibre optics, 20
flexibility, 15, 17, 24, 52
  and performance measures, 50
France, 12, 18

G
Germany, 18, 52, 74, 75, 90
ground rules, 60
groupware, 20
guidelines, 52

H
health and safety standards, 27, 33, 75-8, 91
  checklist, 76
  training, 36
  VDUs, 77

heating, 80, 91
Heimarbeitsgesetz, 74
helplines, 36, 52, 69-70, 78
  technical, 85-6
holiday entitlements, 53
home-based teleworkers, 14
home-working
  assessment of home as workplace, 74-80
  suitability for, 56-8
  traditional, 16, 28-9
hot-desking, 69
hours of work, 24, 36, 65, 90
house moves, 80, 91

I
IBM, 52
India, 14
information-based jobs, 44
information processing, 49
information technology. *see* technology
informed centre, 68
inspections, 75
insurance, 33, 76, 79, 91
interruptions, 23, 42
Ireland, 14
ISDN, 19, 84
isolation, 16, 27, 28, 64
Italy, 18

J
job descriptions, 50-1
job opportunities, 90
jobs, assessment of, 43-5, 50-1

K
key activities, 44

L
launch, 36, 37
legal issues, 33, 36, 74-80
  statutory rights, 90
lighting, 80, 91
loyalty, 27

M
maintenance, 33
management
  change of style, 27
  of communications, 64-71
  improved skills, 24
  issues in teleworking, 48-53
  loss of control, 28, 42, 64
  support essential, 32
  training, 35
managers
  opposition to teleworking, 16
  selection of, 42-3
maternity leave, 90
meeting days, 66
meeting rooms, 68
meetings, regular, 65-6
mentors, 70
mobile phones, 20, 84
modem, 83
mortgage terms, 80

N
NCC survey, 26
neighbourhood office, 22-5

neighbourhood work centres, 14
networks, 66
newsletters, 67
nomad workers, 84
nomadic staff, 14, 49
notice, 90

O

office life
  social aspects, 56-7
office space, 23, 27, 68-9
  problems of, 23
  shared, 14
organizations, local, 61
orientation, 35-6
output measures, 37, 49-50
overheads, 23, 24, 26
overtime, 90

P

pagers, 20, 84
part-time work, 53
pay, 90
PCs. *see* computers
performance measures, 50, 90
peripatetic groups, 14, 49
personal concerns, 19
personnel department
  assessment of jobs, 44
  and teleworking, 33, 40
personnel issues
  and teleworking, 23
photocopying, 80
piece-working, 16, 28, 49
pilot schemes, 16, 35-7

evaluation of, 36-7
planning regulations, 33, 78-9
policy documents, 37
post, 84
practicality, 57-8
privacy, 74, 75
private networks, 85
procedures, 33
processes, 52
productivity, 15, 23, 28-9
  comparisons, 23-5
  increase in, 42
  measures of, 37, 49-50
profiling, 40
project-based work, 23, 49
protection, 74
public data networks, 84
publicity, 34, 37

Q

quality, 49, 51
quality of life, 15, 19, 24
questionnaires, 34-5, 40, 107-13

R

recruitment, 23, 24, 27, 34-5, 67
relocation, 23, 27
Repetitive Strain Injury, 77
responsibilities, 36, 50-1
  equipment, 33, 90-1
  running costs, 79-80
reviews, 37
rights, protection of, 52
running costs, 79-80
rural regeneration, 19, 24

S

sales department, 48-9
sales force, 51
satellite office, 14
satellites, 19
secretarial staff, 68
security
   of data, 27, 79, 86-7
selection criteria, 33, 34-5, 40-5
   for employees, 40-2
   for jobs, 43-5
   for managers, 42-3
self-discipline, 57
self-employment, 22, 25, 53
short-term contracts, 53
sick leave, 23, 24, 26, 42, 53
skills base, 24, 43
skills shortages, 17, 23
social concerns, 19
social events, 66-7
social life, 56-7
space issues, 68-9
   and teleworking, 23, 27-8
staff retention, 26
stationery, 80
status, loss of, 27, 52-3
statutory rights, 90
STE, 29
stress, 24, 27
   of teleworking, 58
sub-contracting, 53
supervision, 48
support groups, 66
support systems, 33
sweat-shops, 16
systems support, 69-70

T

targets, 50
taxation, 33, 78
team meetings, 65-6
technical skills, 36
technology
   and communications, 64, 68, 71
   enabling teleworking, 15, 19-20
teleconferencing, 20
telecottages, 14
telephones, 19, 83
   call back facilities, 84
   costs of, 80, 91
   importance of, 61, 64
   mobile, 20, 84
   new services, 85
   tied or leased lines, 84
telework
   enabling technology, 15, 19-20
teleworking. *see also* management; selection criteria
   advantages of, 15-6, 23-8
   attitudes to, 15-6
   definition of, 13-5
   description of, 12-5
   disadvantages of, 16, 27-9
   driving forces, 16-20
   interest in by age, 18
   making it work, 60-1
   perceptions of, 56
   problems of, 22-5
   range of jobs, 45

reasons for, 22-9
set-up costs, 28, 85
stages of establishment, 32-7
termination of agreement, 90
terms and conditions, 90-1
tenancy agreements, 80
Thailand, 14
third party liability, 91
time-log, 44
timetables, 36
trade unions
   acceptance of teleworking, 29
   access to teleworkers, 68
   concern on running costs, 80
   concern on status, 52
   loss of representation, 27
   resistance to teleworking, 16, 49
   teleworking regulations, 74
training, 33, 35-6, 43, 53, 91
   health and safety standards, 75
   performance measures, 51
   for teleworkers, 51
travel costs, 80, 91

U

unemployment benefit, 90
United Kingdom, 12, 18, 74, 79, 90
   NCC survey, 26
United States, 17, 90
   environmental concerns, 19

V

VDUs, 77
videophones, 20
videos, 20
virtual organization, 14
voice-mail, 20, 84

W

women
   as home-workers, 26
   part-time work, 53
   and teleworking, 23, 50
word processing, 49, 51
work-related issues
   and teleworking, 23
working conditions, 52
workload problems, 23
workplace
   assessment of home as, 74-80
   definition of, 75

European Foundation for the Improvement of Living and Working Conditions

European guide to teleworking: A framework for action

Luxembourg: Office for Official Publications of the European Communities

1995 – 121 pp. – 14.8 x 21 cm

ISBN 92-826-9286-8

Price (excluding VAT) in Luxembourg: ECU 11.50